TIMESAVER FOR EXA

Practice Tests & Tips

FOR FIRST (FCE)

By Helen Chilton, Lynda Edwards and Jacky Newbrook

SCHOLASTIC

Contents

Practice Test 3

Practice Test 4

Introduction

Who is this book for?

This book is for teachers of students who are preparing for the *Cambridge English: First (FCE)* exam and who require extra practice material for the four tests which make up the exam: Reading & Use of English, Writing, Listening and Speaking. Ideal as a supplement to any First Certificate or upper-intermediate coursebook, the topics and activities reflect those typical of the *Cambridge English: First* exam.

The *Cambridge English: First* exam – an overview

Cambridge English: First is a qualification at upper-intermediate level (Level B2 on the CEFR scale), which is officially recognised by universities, employers and governments around the world. The exam is aimed at learners who want to use English for study at an upper-intermediate level, start working in an English-speaking environment, or live independently in an English-speaking country.

How do I use this book?

This *Timesaver for Exams* contains two different types of material: fourteen Boost Your Grade skills lessons and four authentic Practice Tests.

Boost Your Grade lessons

The fourteen Boost Your Grade lessons provide practice of common challenges which students face in the four parts of the exam. These materials are designed to be used before a Practice Test to develop your students' exam strategies. Students can then go on to apply these skills in the Practice Test. Boost Your Grade lessons offer focused practice of exam sub-skills, such as organising your ideas in an essay (Writing) or identifying attitude (Listening), and practice of specific task types, e.g. dealing with multiple-matching (Reading), or engaging in a discussion (Speaking). Alternatively, the Boost Your Grade materials can be used as stand-alone exam-oriented skills lessons alongside your coursebook. Extra Boost Your Grade lessons are provided to help students prepare for the Listening test, which many students find challenging.

- Boost Your Grade lessons are designed to be teacher-led with clear instructions on the pages, which are all photocopiable.

- The part of the test and the lesson focus are clearly labelled at the top of each lesson.

- This symbol 🕐 indicates the approximate lesson length. (Please note that timings may vary according to class size and language level.)

- Boost your Grade tips provide advice for exam strategy.

- The comprehensive answer key gives full explanation of the answers.

- Some activities include pairwork to generate more language and encourage students to engage more fully with the task. These can be adapted depending on context and class size.

The *Cambridge English: First* exam consists of four tests as follows:

TEST	TIMING	PARTS	FORMAT
READING & USE OF ENGLISH	1 hour 15 minutes	7	Parts 1 to 4 contain tasks with a grammar or vocabulary focus. Parts 5 to 7 contain a range of texts with accompanying reading comprehension tasks.
WRITING	1 hour 20 minutes	2	Part 1 is a compulsory discursive essay. In Part 2, students choose from three different task types which can include an article, an informal or formal email / letter, a review or a report.
LISTENING	approx. 40 minutes	4	Parts 1 and 4 are multiple-choice, Part 2 involves sentence completion and Part 3 is a multiple matching task.
SPEAKING	14 minutes	4	Tasks: a short exchange with the interlocutor, a one-minute individual 'long turn', a collaborative task with a fellow candidate and a discussion.

Practice Tests

This *Timesaver for Exams* provides four complete and authentic-level Practice Tests with answer key for all four tests of the exam. Depending on your students' needs, you can use the Practice Tests in this *Timesaver for Exams* to target particular parts of the test or to set up a mock test. The Practice Tests are annotated with 'Think it through' tips and Boost Your Grade activities to provide support for students. The tips aim to help students identify and avoid common mistakes and to help them build strategies for exam success. Practice Tests 3 & 4 contain less support in order to increase students' autonomy and provide a more authentic exam experience.

How do I set up an authentic Listening Practice Test?

The complete Listening Practice Tests each take about forty minutes. Make photocopies of the Practice Test question sheets as well as the answer sheet on page 143 for each of your students. During the actual test, students will hear each listening extract twice. On the CDs that accompany this *Timesaver for Exams*, the short dialogues in Part 1 are each recorded twice. Parts 2–4 are not repeated on the CD and you will need to play each track again for your students. This symbol 🎧 indicates the relevant track on the accompanying CDs. As in the exam, time is given on each recording for the students to read each question before they listen. Emphasise to your students the importance of using this time. At the end of the exam give students five minutes to copy their answers onto the answer sheet.

How important is exam strategy to exam success?

The Boost Your Grade lessons and Practice Tests in this *Timesaver for Exams* will support teachers and help learners prepare adequately for the exam. The *Cambridge English: First* exam is a challenging exam requiring students to demonstrate a language level of B2 on the CEFR scale. The top grade in the exam (grade A) is equivalent to C1 on the CEFR scale. Familiarity with each part of the exam is essential for students to be able to perform at their best. Practice of discrete exam task types helps students to develop fundamental skills such as note-taking and listening or reading for relevant information. In addition, practice tests can help students prepare by giving them a chance to focus on maintaining concentration, time management and coping with anxiety. These skills are crucial for all exam students, whatever their level.

The Timesaver series

The Timesaver series provides hundreds of ready-made lessons for all language levels and age groups, covering skills work, language practice and cross-curricular and cross-cultural material. See the full range of print and digital resources at: **www.scholastic.co.uk/elt**

40 mins

How to ... express things in different ways

1 **Work in pairs. Match the phrases that have a similar meaning.**

1 I think you should …
2 I'm very sorry that I …
3 I find it easy to …
4 I wish I had …
5 You mustn't forget …
6 It's certainly true …
7 He always arrives late …
8 I may not be able to …
9 It's common knowledge that …
10 She was allowed to …
11 It's possible it's not right …
12 She took no notice of …

a) She paid no attention to …
b) It's possible that I can't …
c) I advise you to …
d) I need to remind you …
e) He never turns up on time …
f) I apologise for …
g) I have no difficulty in …
h) It must be correct …
i) I regret that I …
j) It could be false …
k) Everyone knows that …
l) They let her …

2 **Change the underlined part of each sentence using a phrase from exercise 1. Do not change the meaning. Make any other changes so that the sentence is grammatically correct.**

Example:

a) I need to remind you to phone Tom,

   You mustn't forget to phone Tom.

b) Mary always arrives late – it's so annoying!

c) Did you hear that John's parents let him drive the family car?

d) 'I think you should do your homework more carefully!' said the teacher

e) I may not be able to come to your party – I'll have to let you know.

f) I wish I had studied harder last year!

> **Boost your grade!**
>
> In Part 4 you have to complete a sentence so that it has a similar meaning to another sentence, using a given word. You use between two and five words. You need to think about:
> - grammar e.g. passives, reported speech
> - vocabulary and collocations e.g. phrasal verbs, fixed phrases

3a **Work in pairs. Read the exam task on page 7 that a student has completed. Which two answers are correct?**

3b **Now match the mistakes to the sentences in the exam task in exercise 4.**

The student has:

a) used too many words
b) changed the key word
c) made a grammatical mistake
d) made a mistake with the expression/idiom
e) made a spelling mistake
f) sentences don't mean the same

> **Boost your grade!**
>
> Remember that contractions count as two words e.g. *don't = do not*

✏ Exam task

4 Complete the exam task, then check your answers with a partner.

Complete the second sentence so that it has a similar meaning to the first sentence, using the word given. Use between two and five words, including the word given.

1 There were so many people at the concert that I couldn't find my friend.
crowded

The concert ......*was so crowded that*...... I couldn't find my friend.

2 I only went to see the film because you said it was good!
recommended

If ...*you had not recommended the film*... I would not have gone to see it!

3 'Why don't we go out on Saturday?' said Chris.
suggested

Chris ......*suggested to go out*...... on Saturday.

4 I definitely don't remember turning the light off.
forgotten

I .....*may have forgotten to turn*..... the light off.

5 Rosemary can sing much better than me.
well

I .....*can't sing as well*..... as Rosemary.

6 You will only succeed if you work harder.
unless

You ......*won't suceed unless*...... you work harder.

7 I always find it hard to choose what to eat!
decision

I always find it hard ......*to do a decision*...... about what to eat!

8 My sister regrets not having taken the job when she had the chance.
wishes

My sister ......*wished she had taken*...... the job when she had the chance.

Checklist for Part 4

Check that:

✓ both sentences mean exactly the same

✓ you have used the key word and have **not** changed it

✓ you have **not** written more than five words

✓ your spelling is correct

60 mins

How to ... organise your ideas in an essay

1 **Which statement about essays is <u>not</u> true?**

An essay:

a) has an introduction and a clear conclusion

b) uses informal and colourful language to engage readers

c) presents a point of view

d) uses connecting words to organise ideas

2 **Work in pairs. Read the exam task and answer the questions.**

a) Do the two points given in the exam task support the statement?

b) Think of examples to support the first two points.

Boost your grade!

Remember to add a third point of your own, which should be different from the two points you are given. You will not get a good mark if you forget this.

✎ Exam task

In your English class you have been talking about whether it's a good idea for young people to travel for a year before they go to university or start work. Now, your English teacher has asked you to write an essay.

Some people say it's a good idea for young people to travel for a year before they go to university or start work. Do you agree?

Notes
Write about:

1. having new experiences

2. learning languages

3. .... (your own idea)

3 **Read the Boost your grade! and choose the best idea for the third point in the exam task. Then think of an example to support it.**

a) needing to save money

b) meeting new people

c) having fun

Boost your grade!

If the notes given support the statement, try to think of one that puts the opposite point of view.

4 **Read two possible introductions to the exam task and choose the best one.**

A Many young people choose to travel before they start university or take a job, but is this really a good idea? There are arguments for and against it, and it's not always an easy decision to make.

B Travelling round the world is a great idea for young people and it gives them lots of new things to learn and to experience. It's even better when they travel before university because they have plenty of time to waste, and they can make the most of every opportunity.

5 **Read the next three paragraphs of the essay and choose the best linking words.**

(1) *Firstly / although / so*, it is a wonderful opportunity for young people to have new experiences which they cannot have while they are at school. They can **(2)** *also / too / next* learn to become independent, which is an extra bonus.

(3) *On the one hand / Secondly / Even*, they will have the chance to learn new languages while they travel, which is not only interesting but will be useful for them in the future. **(4)** *In case / In addition / After all*, it is a global world nowadays and they will meet and work with people from many different countries.

(5) *Also / On the other hand / Consequently*, many young people think that it is more important to save money. If they go travelling for a year they will spend money, instead of saving it, which they could do if they stayed at home. **(6)** *For this reason / Because / But* they may prefer not to travel for such a long time, **(7)** *because / since / although* they may still think it is worth travelling for a few months and working for the rest of the time.

6 **Now read two possible conclusions to the exam task and choose the best one.**

A I think that travelling is always fun, and I would love to do it if I could even if it is expensive.

B Although there are arguments on both sides, on balance it is a good idea for young people to travel before going to university or starting work.

> **Boost your grade!**
>
> Your conclusion should be a logical ending to your essay and remember to include your own opinion.

7 **Read the complete essay. How is it organised? Put these sections into the order they appear in the essay.**

.... Third own idea (against)

....*1*..... Introduction

.... First given idea (for)

.... Conclusion

.... Second given idea (for)

> **Boost your grade!**
>
> Always support all your ideas with examples.
> Remember there is no right answer to the question.

8 **Now write your own answer to the task.**

9 **Read through your answer and use the checklist to make sure your essay is clear and your ideas are well-organised.**

Checklist for Part 1

Have you:

✓ included both points from the task in your essay?

✓ added an idea of your own?

✓ used one paragraph for each point?

✓ used connectors to link your ideas clearly?

✓ included an introduction and a conclusion?

How to ... deal with multiple choice questions

1 Work in pairs. Match the words in the box to the question type. The words can be used more than once.

> agreement   detail   emotion   opinion/attitude
> purpose in speaking   topic

a) How does the woman feel about the match?   *emotion*

b) What does the man think about the programme?

c) What is the subject of the man's talk?

d) What do they agree about?

e) Where does the man want to meet his friend?

f) What is the woman's attitude towards the plan?

g) What does the teacher want her students to do first?

h) What is the television programme about?

i) What do they both think?

j) What is the man doing when he speaks?

> **Boost your grade!**
>
> In Part 1 you listen to short monologues or dialogues. You may be asked about:
>
> - a speaker's attitude, opinion or feeling
> - why they are speaking
> - what they are talking about
> - details of things such as the location of the speakers
> - what the speakers agree about

✏ Exam task

2a Work in pairs. Read the exam task. What is it testing? Choose a word from the box in exercise 1.

You will hear two friends talking about a television programme they have seen. What did the woman think about the programme?

A   It was more interesting than she had expected.

B   She would like to see more programmes like this.

C   It was worth seeing several times.

2b 🎧 Now listen and choose the correct answer.

2c 📄 Work in pairs. Read the transcript on page 118. Underline the part which gave you the answer.

3a Work in pairs. Read the exam task. What is it testing?

You hear a teacher talking to her students. What is she doing?

A   describing a difficult homework project

B   criticising some earlier work

C   explaining how to do some research

3b 🎧 Now listen and choose the correct answer.

3c 📄 Work in pairs. Read the transcript on page 118. Underline the part which gave you the answer.

4   **Read the conversations. Do the speakers agree or disagree with each other?**

a)   Man: I think people should be able to use their phones anywhere they like.

Woman: They can be distracting in quiet places like libraries.

b)   Man: People aren't very polite to each other these days.

Woman: No-one holds the door open for you, and sometimes they don't even say thank you!

c)   Man: It's much better to travel by bus than by car.

Woman: It's cheaper, too.

d)   Woman: Talent shows are a great way to discover new singers and dancers.

Man: They're just a waste of time. Really good singers will always succeed.

e)   Man: It's good that supermarkets charge for plastic bags.

Woman: Well, things are expensive enough without adding that on top.

f)   Woman: Children should be taught practical skills at school.

Man: Learning to decorate a room and put up shelves would certainly be useful.

✏ Exam task

5a   **Read the exam task.**

You hear two friends talking about travelling round their town. What do they agree about?

A   the cost of public transport

B   the difficulty of parking

C   the need to have a pedestrian zone

> **Boost your grade!**
>
> Use the time you are given to read the questions and the options carefully, so you're prepared for what you'll hear and know what's being tested.

5b   🎧 **Now listen and choose the correct answer.**

5c   📄 **Work in pairs. Read the transcript on page 118. Underline the part that gave you the answer.**

How to ... manage both parts of the long turn

1 **Read the exam task on page 13. Which two things should you <u>not</u> do?**

a) compare the pictures

b) describe the pictures in detail

c) speculate about the question

d) give your own opinion of the photographs

2a **Work in pairs. Match the statements to the correct picture by adding *He, She* or *Both* in each gap.**

a) … is buying a snack in a café, and there are other people sitting in the same place.

b … is buying food from a local shop.

c) … is buying fruit and checking it for quality by smelling it.

d … seems to be hungry and not bothered about buying healthy food.

e) … is inside a large, modern place.

f) … is outside a rather old-fashioned shop in a street where there are parked cars.

g) … seem to be unstressed and relaxed.

2b **Think of two more statements about each picture and one more about both.**

2c **Use the words in the box to link the statements and compare the pictures.**

> although   both   but   conversely   on the other hand   though   whereas

Example: In the top picture the man has just paid for his food and drink, whereas in the bottom picture the woman is still trying to decide what to buy.

> **Boost your grade!**
>
> Don't just describe the pictures – compare them using linking words.

3 **Speculating about the question. Work in pairs.**

a) Think of five different places where people choose to buy food.

b) Think of two reasons why people choose to buy food in each place.

Example: Supermarket. People buy food there because there's a lot of choice.

4 **Look at the pictures again and think of two reasons why each person has decided to buy food in these places.**

5 🎧 **Now listen to a student doing the task. Does she**

a) describe the pictures in detail?

b) compare the pictures and then answer the question?

c) answer the question before comparing the pictures?

d) forget to answer the question at all?

6 **What two reasons does she give for why the people have decided to buy food in these places?**

a) quality and freshness   b) speed   c) price

✏ Exam task Part 2

Your photographs show people buying food in different places. Compare the photographs and say why you think the people have decided to buy food in these places.

7   **Work in pairs. Take it in turns to give your own answer to the task. You should spend about 30 seconds comparing the pictures and 30 seconds answering the question.**

Boost your grade!

Keep talking so that you fill the minute - it doesn't matter if the examiner stops you before you have finished.

After your partner has spoken about their pictures, you will be asked a question about them, so you must listen to your partner.

READING AND USE OF ENGLISH

Part 1

For questions **1–8**, read the text below and decide which answer (**A**, **B**, **C** or **D**) best fits each gap. There is an example at the beginning **(0)**.

Mark your answers **on the separate answer sheet**.

0	**A** imagination	**B** reputation	**C** story	**D** belief

0	A ▢	B ▬	C ▢	D ▢

The sloth

The sloth, an animal from central and South America has the **(0)** .... of being one of the laziest animals on Earth. These cute **(1)** ...., with their big black eyes, **(2)** .... most of their lives in the treetops, coming down to the ground just once a week. When they are in the treetops they can't be **(3)** .... by predators. They spend hours hanging upside **(4)** ...., their claws clinging tightly to the branches. Almost every activity is **(5)** .... out in this position, including sleeping, because it uses the least energy. Under the branches the sloths look just like a **(6)** .... of leaves. An insect called the sloth moth helps **(7)** .... the sloth's fur green so it can hide from eagles looking for food. If they are ever caught on the ground it is impossible for sloths to **(8)** .... a predator, so they have to depend on their strong, sharp claws and then the lazy sloth will fight for its life.

1	**A** organisms	**B** persons	**C** creatures	**D** beings
2	**A** pass	**B** spend	**C** wait	**D** exist
3	**A** arrived	**B** moved	**C** reached	**D** searched
4	**A** down	**B** off	**C** out	**D** away
5	**A** done	**B** continued	**C** carried	**D** sorted
6	**A** line	**B** pile	**C** range	**D** type
7	**A** let	**B** make	**C** allow	**D** force
8	**A** run	**B** leave	**C** break	**D** escape

THINK IT THROUGH

Always read the text all the way through first, ignoring the gaps, to get the general idea of what it is about.

Part 2

For questions **9–16**, read the text below and think of the word which best fits each gap. Use only one word in each gap. There is an example at the beginning **(0)**.

Write your answers **IN CAPITAL LETTERS on the separate answer sheet**.

Example: | 0 | H | A | S | | | | | | | | | | | | | | |

A lot of marathons

Ben Smith **(0)** .... just finished an incredible

challenge. He made the decision **(9)** .... year to

run 401 marathons in 401 days to raise £250,000 for anti-bullying

charities. **These (10)** .... place in 309 locations

around the UK. His plan was to finish on 9th October and for a

while it looked **(11)** .... if that goal would not be

achieved. Several months **(12)** .... **starting** he had

to take 11 days off to rest after severe back problems. However,

when he was back **(13)** .... his feet he pledged

to run extra miles every day for the rest of the marathons.

(14) .... his record-breaking challenge he also

visited over 90 schools to **(15)** .... talks about

bullying and raising awareness of the problem. He also inspired

thousands of people to run a marathon with him; for five hundred

of these it was the first marathon they **(16)** ....

ever run. Ben burned over 2.5 million calories and got through

22 pairs of trainers!

Think about what part of speech follows 'these'.

Consider what type of word 'starting' is as that will help you decide what might go before it.

THINK IT THROUGH

Remember to read the whole sentence after filling in the gap to check that it makes sense.

Part 3

For questions **17–24**, read the text below. Use the word given in capitals at the end of some of the lines to form a word that fits in the gap in the same line. There is an example at the beginning **(0)**.

Write your answers **IN CAPITAL LETTERS on the separate answer sheet**.

Example: | 0 | E | C | O | N | O | M | I | S | T | | | | | | | |

Are we better off?

According to a report by an **(0)** .... , a lot of thirty-year	**ECONOMY**
olds think they're less **(17)** .... than those in their forties	**WEALTH**
and this may be true. We tend to think that generations get	
(18) .... richer because of higher salaries, more	**INCREASE**
(19) .... between food suppliers and so on, and the	**COMPETE**
salaries of today's thirty-year olds are certainly **(20)**	**COMPARE**
to those of older earners.	
So, why are they poorer? There are several reasons. The high cost	
of university tuition fees means students start their working lives with	
a lot of debt. **(21)** .... is another issue. Buying a	**ACCOMMODATE**
house is now very expensive and many people rent instead.	
An **(22)** .... point is that today's generation are	**ADDITION**
enjoying the money they earn rather than saving it – quite	
(23) .... in today's economic climate. But without	**UNDERSTAND**
savings or a home to sell on your **(24)** .... life could	**RETIRE**
be very hard in the future.	

 THINK IT THROUGH

Identify the type of word you need to form by looking at the sentence structure. In the example 'O' the word before the gap is an article. This tells you that the word in the gap must be a noun.

Part 4

For questions **25–30**, complete the second sentence so that it has a similar meaning to the first sentence, using the word given. **Do not change the word given.** You must use between **two** and **five** words including the word given. Here is an example **(0)**.

Example:

0 It's fine for students to eat in the classrooms at lunchtime.

   ALLOWED

   Students ....*are allowed to*.................... eat in the classrooms at lunchtime.

___

25 We should finish this rehearsal soon, because they usually close the building at 8.30.

   SUPPOSED

   We should finish this rehearsal soon, as .... close the building at 8.30.

26 Is it **necessary** for us to give in our homework this afternoon? ○┄┄┄┄

   HAVE

   Do .... give in our homework this afternoon?

> What other ways do you know to talk about necessity?

27 If we don't leave now we'll miss the train.

   UNLESS

   We'll miss the train .... now.

28 I really **hate** waiting in queues. ○┄┄┄┄┄┄┄┄┄┄┄┄

   STAND

   I .... in queues.

> What other ways do you know to say 'I hate'?

29 We need more sandwiches than this.

   ENOUGH

   There .... sandwiches for all of us.

30 Brian refused to leave until he'd finished the game.

   INSISTED

   Brian .... before he left.

Part 5

You are going to read part of a story in which a young girl talks about a competition. For questions **31–36** choose the answer (**A**, **B**, **C** or **D**) which you think fits best according to the text.

Mark your answers **on the separate answer sheet**.

A long afternoon

Ella couldn't believe how quickly the day had come round. It hardly seemed a moment since she had taken a deep breath and sent her email to apply for the competition. And yet, here she was, waiting to be called up onto the stage. Too fast, too sudden, her thudding heart was telling her but she knew that however long, however many more weeks she could have had – it would never have been long enough to prepare for this, her moment in the spotlight. It was her time and she couldn't run from it.

She had always sung. According to her mother she sang before struggling up on to two legs to walk. And also, according to her mother, it had been her inspiration that had nurtured her daughter's amazing talent. It was Sara who had played the music that Ella had loved, danced to and copied. In fact it was extraordinary that Sara hadn't taken the credit for Ella's courage to actually apply in the first place. She was always boastful of being the inspiration behind everything else her daughter achieved. But this, this being here at this time, shaking with fear and desperately regretting that crazy decision, was all down to Ella herself. The fact that Sara was sitting next to her, eyeing up the opposition and commenting on the clothes choices of the other contestants, was NOT Ella's choice at all.

She slumped back into her chair, wishing the floor could swallow her up, as her mother made yet another loud comment about the amount of make-up evident in the room. She looked up again at the huge mirror on the wall that reflected back the crowds of nervous, shifting people filling every chair at every table in the big room. She tried to shut out the chatter but it was impossible, like a buzzing insect going round and round your head. The air was getting increasingly heavier and thicker with cheap perfume and the heat of people squashed together. Ella felt the room start to turn a little and she wondered if she were going to faint, but then a dig from her mother's fingers on her leg made her sit up.

'Did you hear that?' Sara asked, referring to the previous singer on the stage whose final words were fading from the loudspeaker that brought the performances into the room. Her mouth lifted at the corners in a small satisfied smile. 'What was she thinking of? Terrible song, terrible voice. Ella – you'll win this easily.' And she looked round the room defiantly as if someone was about to challenge her. Suddenly there was silence. The room was holding its collective breath. Who was up next? The girl in black came down the stairs with her list in her hand. She had a microphone linked to a pair of headphones that pushed her fair hair back from her face. Her eyes scanned the names and the silence continued. Fifty pairs of eyes watched her lips form the next name. 'Ella Golding?' she said and the chatter resumed.

It was Sara who responded. 'Here!' she said importantly. 'Here, this is Ella Golding,' and added unnecessarily, 'I'm her mother.' She pushed Ella to her feet and followed as Ella walked unsteadily to the stairs. A black arm reached out in front of her firmly. 'I'm sorry, only contestants from this point.' And at last Ella breathed. She climbed the stairs, finally alone, and stood at the side of the stage. The lights were bright and the audience was dark and waiting. For a moment she stood quietly, savouring the sensation of being there and then her music began, and she walked out with confidence, her nerves left behind with her mother.

31 In the first paragraph Ella is feeling

  A self-critical that she hadn't done enough preparation.

  B surprised that she had had the courage to apply.

  C apprehensive about her upcoming performance.

  D regretful that she had not taken this step before.

32 What do we learn about Ella's mother in paragraph two?

  A She was responsible for Ella entering the competition.

  B She has passed on her singing ability to her daughter.

  C She is concerned about how well her daughter will perform.

  D She believes she has played a great part in Ella's development.

33 What contributes to making Ella feel ill?

  A the atmosphere in the room

  B excessive noise in the room

  C the presence of flies in the room

  D her own nervousness

34 What does the phrase 'holding its collective breath' imply in paragraph 4?

  A the air in the room wasn't fresh

  B the people in the room were waiting for news

  C the administrators were gathering information from the contestants

  D the contestants were doing breathing exercises

35 Which adjective describes Ella's mother in paragraph 4?

  A aggressive

  B misinformed

  C constructively critical

  D confident

36 What impression are we left with at the end of the story?

  A Ella had been in this situation many times before.

  B Ella was relieved when she was on her own.

  C Ella was likely to win the competition.

  D Ella was reluctant to leave her mother.

THINK IT THROUGH

Read each question and find the part of the text it refers to. Then reread that section of the text carefully.

Part 6

You are going to read an article about whether teenagers should do extreme sports. Six sentences have been removed from the article. Choose from the sentences **A–G** the one which fits each gap (**37–42**). There is one extra sentence you do not need to use.

Mark your answers **on the separate answer sheet**.

Should teens do extreme sports?

Extreme sports are popular with many age groups but there are many controversies around whether teens in particular should be encouraged to participate in sports like these. Some see them as far too dangerous for teenage bodies which are perhaps not yet fully developed. **37** I have to say that I totally agree with the latter. Taking risks is a way of teaching yourself bravery and stepping outside your comfort zone to do something that scares you can make you feel empowered — even if you don't get it right the first time. A study recently found that conquering physical feats that scare you (for example, surfing a big wave) can transform your overall confidence. That's why extreme sports are perfect for teens, who are eager to learn and perfect new passions.

I've been snowboarding since I was nine years old, and I've loved every bit of the sport since. Being on the slopes for hours a day helped me gain an understanding of the way my body works. **38** Snowboarding taught me how to push myself, especially when I was scared of falling. And it made me more persistent because one way or another, I always have to make it to the bottom of the slope.

I believe every teen should be able to experience those benefits, and many more. All sports, especially extreme ones, require physical exertion, which keeps you in great shape. And, because it must be noted, the adrenaline rush from an extreme sport is much healthier than the high that some teenagers might seek from unhealthy activities such as drug use. There's nothing quite like that feeling you get as you're about to descend a steep slope or lift off for a complicated jump. It's adrenaline that is produced by our bodies when we're confronted by a frightening situation and prepares us to face a danger or run from it, fight or flight. That's what attracts teens to extreme sports. **39**

I know there are people who doubt the benefits. Their main argument is that, as we all know, the teen brain is particularly keen on thrill-seeking and not so good at evaluating risk. **40** If we don't take risks, we don't learn!

Even the best extreme athletes get hurt sometimes. **41** It's true that there are many injuries every year, with skateboarding being the main culprit. But it's all about being trained well and having the right equipment. It's fair to say that a certain amount of risk is involved and these sports will never be injury free, but good preparation can reduce the likelihood of accidents if not rule them out completely. Fear of injury shouldn't prevent teens from participating in a sport they enjoy. With a helmet and proper padding (and some patience!), they'll minimise the chance of injury and benefit from all the great things extreme sports have to offer. If they never try, they'll never know how good they could become.

42 An extreme sport can teach us patience, control, and discipline, and it might even become an activity that we fall in love with in the process.

A They also introduce you to a positive community of people who share the same interests.

B They are always willing to help you improve.

C Adults need to stop doubting teenagers so much!

D I learned which muscles are responsible for which movements, how to adjust my technique to avoid injury, and what my physical limitations are.

E But surely this is part of growing up and in fact part of human development!

F Others view them as a perfect hobby for adventurous teenagers.

G Those against the idea of teens doing extreme sports talk up the dangerous side of it.

Boost your grade!

1 Read the instructions to this Part 6 task carefully and then look at the title and the photograph. What opinions do you think might be given in the article?

2 Skim the text and match each idea with the correct paragraph.

Paragraph 1	**a)** the possible dangers and safety precautions
Paragraph 2	**b)** why teenagers should be allowed to take chances
Paragraph 3	**c)** different views on extreme sports
Paragraph 4	**d)** what we can learn from extreme sports
Paragraph 5	**e)** the social and physical advantages of extreme sports
Paragraph 6	**f)** the writer's personal experience

3a Now look at sentences A-G again. Which of the sentences talk about the following ideas?

a) the possible dangers and safety precautions

c) different views on extreme sports

e) the social and physical advantages of extreme sports

f) the writer's personal experience

3b Does looking for contextual clues help you to match some of the sentences?

Part 7

You are going read about four memorable journeys. For questions **43–52** choose from the sections (**A–D**). The sections may be chosen more than once.

Mark your answers **on the separate answer sheet**.

Which section mentions

a journey that the passengers had prepared for?	**43**
something that might have been <u>enjoyable</u> at a different time?	**44**
how a health risk was averted?	**45**
a <u>spectacular</u> visual effect?	**46**
a journey that involved two forms of transport?	**47**
an unexpectedly <u>good consequence</u> of a bad journey?	**48**
an event that wasn't as memorable as it should have been?	**49**
a period when people didn't know what was happening?	**50**
a journey that was <u>memorable</u> because of another person's experience?	**51**
an <u>unawareness</u> of a potentially dangerous situation?	**52**

Boost your grade!

The words used in the options will NOT be the same as those used in the text(s). A student has underlined some words in the options. Before you read the texts, think of synonyms for the following words and phrases:

a) enjoyable   **c)** a good consequence   **e)** be unaware

b) spectacular   **d)** find something memorable

Now read the texts. What synonyms for these words appear in the texts?

A At the age of 11 I was a ballet fanatic and my parents had decided to take me to a performance of *The Nutcracker* in London for my birthday. This meant leaving our car at the station and a long train journey there and back. I should remember more about the ballet, but that was blanked out by the eventful journey home. Snow had started falling while we were in the theatre and developed into a full-blown blizzard while we were on the train. The drive home from the station was a nightmare for my poor dad. We all hung on tightly as the car skidded up and down a steep hill – the roads didn't get salted in those days – passing others who had broken down; we dared not stop to help them. Needless to say I was thoroughly entertained by the whole adventure, not realising how close we'd been to crashing!

B An extra night on the Caribbean island of Barbados might seem a fantastic idea, but for the passengers travelling on a return flight to the UK a few years ago it certainly wasn't. I was flying home after two glorious weeks in the sun when the flight had to return to the airport 15 minutes into the journey. Apparently someone had discovered something unusual in a seat pocket and for safety reasons we had to turn back. The flight crew then ran out of air hours and couldn't work any longer and after a frustrating four-hour wait at the airport, we had to spend the night at a nearby hotel. The only bonus was that after complaining about the total lack of communication during the delay I got an upgrade to First Class on my next trip out there!

C Long plane journeys can be very tiring, especially for children. When my son was very young we flew to New Zealand to stay with relatives and it was hard to keep him occupied. The return flight was overnight but unfortunately he couldn't sleep – perhaps it was the excitement. So, there we were James and I, the only passengers awake on the whole plane (my wife was snoring beside us) when up comes the flight attendant. She asked whether James might enjoy a visit to the cockpit. Of course, he jumped at the chance and before long we were with the pilot looking out into the night sky. What an incredible moment. The sky was filled with amazing colours – the southern lights – they stretched right across the sky. My son couldn't believe his eyes and my lasting memory of that moment is not of the lights but of the expression on his young face.

D About three years ago we were on our way to Scotland. It was going to be a long journey and the kids were really young then, so we'd packed a lot of games and music to play in the car. Suddenly there were red tail lights up ahead and we stopped. I'm not exaggerating – we didn't move for four hours; the motorway was completely blocked with traffic both in front and behind us. We learned from the radio that a big lorry had just crashed into one of the motorway bridges. Luckily no one was hurt but it meant four hours sitting motionless in traffic. It was a very hot summer's day and the police motorbikes drove up and down handing out water to everyone to prevent dehydration. It wasn't a very good beginning to the holiday but the kids went to sleep and we eventually got moving again.

WRITING

Part 1

You **must** answer this question. Write your answer in **140–190** words in an appropriate style on the separate answer sheet.

---

1   In your English class you have been talking about whether reading newspapers is the best way to find out about the news. Now, your English teacher has asked you to write an essay.

Write your essay using **all** the notes and giving reasons for your point of view.

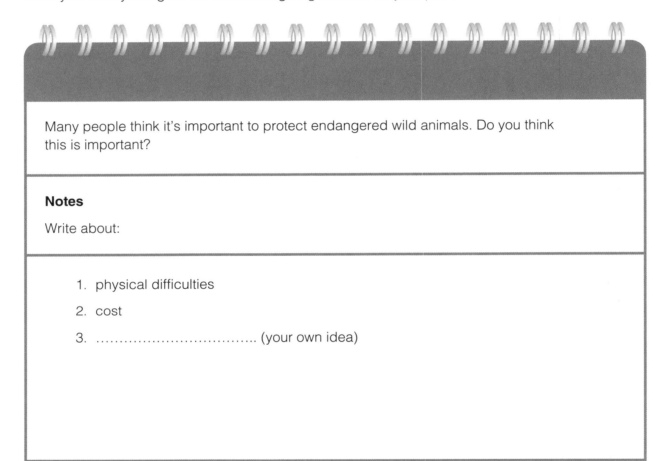

Many people think it's important to protect endangered wild animals. Do you think this is important?

Notes

Write about:

1. physical difficulties

2. cost

3. ……………………………….. (your own idea)

THINK IT THROUGH

Remember to include both the points you are given, and add one of your own. It's a good idea to use a separate paragraph for each, so that you have shown how your essay is organised.

Part 2

Write an answer to one of the questions **2–4** in this part. Write your answer in **140–190** words in an appropriate style on the separate answer sheet. Put the question number in the box at the top of the answer sheet.

---

2 You see this announcement in an English-language magazine.

> **Articles wanted**
>
> ### The best holiday I have ever had
>
> What was the best holiday you have ever had? Where did you go? What did you do? Why was it so good?
>
> Write us an article answering these questions.
>
> We will print the most interesting articles in our magazine.

Write your **article**.

3 You have received this email from your English-speaking friend Jo.

> **From:** Jo
>
> **Subject:** Your move
>
> Hi! I haven't heard from you since you moved to your new house, so I'd love to know what you think of it. How does it compare with your old house? Are there things to do in that part of town?
>
> Let me know how you're getting on!
>
> Jo

Write your **email**.

 Email: Remember you are writing to a friend and you must answer their questions. Use informal language.

4
> You recently visited a new museum in your town. Now your teacher has asked you to write a report for your class on the new museum.
>
> Your report should:
>
> - include information about what you could see in the museum
>
> - give reasons why the museum was good or bad
>
> - say whether you would recommend the museum, and why

Write your **report**.

LISTENING

Part 1

 You will hear people talking in eight different situations. For questions **1–8**, choose the best answer (**A**, **B**, or **C**).

---

1   You hear a woman telling her friend about going on an environmentally-friendly holiday. What was she surprised about?

   A   how peaceful the resort was

   B   how interesting the surroundings were

   C   how comfortable the accommodation was

2   You hear **two** friends talking about taking part in a maths competition. What do they agree about it?

   A   It went on for too long.

   B   The prize wasn't very interesting.

   C   The questions were too challenging.

> Make sure **both** speakers have the same opinion about the option you choose.

3   You hear a woman talking about summer camps for young people in America. What is she doing?

   A   providing details about camp activities

   B   persuading listeners to sign up for a camp

   C   explaining why the camps are so successful

4   You hear two friends talking about a TV programme they have seen. What do they **both** say about it?

   A   It raised some interesting points for discussion.

   B   It made them question their behaviour.

   C   It motivated them to take action.

> Make sure **both** friends talk about this aspect of the TV programme.

THINK IT THROUGH

Each of the eight questions in this part of the test includes a description of the situation followed by a comprehension question. These questions may focus on gist, feelings and attitude or detail. Read the question carefully to make sure you listen for the correct information.

5   You hear a girl talking to her father about kindness.
        What does she say?

   A   She will try to be kinder to others.

   B   The reason for being kind is unimportant.

   C   Some people have no real desire to help others.

6   You hear a young woman talking about her job in a supermarket.
        How does she feel about it?

   A   keen to earn extra money when she can

   B   interested in the opportunities for promotion

   C   surprised by how much knowledge she's acquired

What phrases might the woman use to talk about earning extra money, opportunities for promotion or knowledge?

7   You hear a girl talking about some volunteering work with elephants she is going to do.
        How does she feel about it?

   A   anxious about doing the wrong thing

   B   determined to be as helpful as possible

   C   confident in her knowledge of the animals

8   You hear two friends talking about a football match they have just watched.
        What does the girl say about it?

   A   She was disappointed to miss seeing a goal.

   B   She thought the team played well.

   C   She enjoyed the atmosphere.

What words or phrases might the girl use to express her disappointment, her approval or her enjoyment?

Part 2

 You will hear a boy called Matt talking about an outdoor activity weekend he took part in.

For questions **9–18**, complete the sentences with a word or short phrase.

Outdoor activity weekend

 THINK IT THROUGH

You will have 45 seconds to read the text before you listen to the Part 2 recording. Read each of the sentences and think about what kind of word is missing, e.g. noun, adjective, etc. Look at the words before **and** after the gap.

Matt heard about the activity centre from his **(9)** ....

Matt hadn't been expecting to sleep in a **(10)** ....

Matt's group decided to call themselves the **(11)** ....

Matt's team was disappointed not to be given any **(12)** .... when they cooked dinner.

In the first activity, the groups had to rely on a **(13)** .... to find their way.

During the task, one of the boys in Matt's group thought he had heard a **(14)** ....

On the hike they went on, the groups acquired what Matt calls **(15)** .... skills.

When they played a climbing game, participants had to try to touch a **(16)** ....

Matt uses the word '**(17)** ....' to describe his singing ability.

The final activity of the stay was intended to help participants deal with their **(18)** ....

Part 3

 You will hear five short extracts in which people are talking about women they know who inspire them. For questions **19–23**, choose from the list (**A–H**) what each speaker says about the woman who inspires them. Use the letters only once. There are three extra letters which you do not need to use.

THINK IT THROUGH

You may hear other ideas from the list mentioned, but only **one** option correctly answers the question for each speaker.

A	She is very talented.	
B	She gives good advice.	
C	She has a lot of patience.	
D	She believes in my abilities.	
E	She is an excellent listener.	
F	She is always honest with me.	
G	She has a great sense of humour.	
H	She is positive about her situation.	

Speaker 1		19
Speaker 2		20
Speaker 3		21
Speaker 4		22
Speaker 5		23

Boost your grade!

The words you hear may be different from the words you read, but they will have a similar meaning. What phrases did you hear that helped you answer the questions?

 Look at the transcript on page 120 and check your answers in the key.

Part 4

 You will hear an interview with a woman called Ruth Brown, who is talking about online friendships. For questions **24–30**, choose the best answer (**A**, **B**, or **C**).

---

24   What does Ruth say when asked about online friendships?

   A   It's difficult to give proper advice by text.

   B   Friends have more contact online than face-to-face.

   C   Virtual friendships can be as satisfying as real-life ones.

25   What is Ruth's opinion about posting online?

   A   It is easier to be honest.

   B   It can be harder to say positive things about friends.

   C   The effects of comments on others should be considered.

26   Ruth says that meeting people online

   A   offers a wider friend base than it would elsewhere in life.

   B   means gaining access to people with similar interests.

   C   is much easier to do than in real-life situations.

27   How does Ruth feel about her online friends?

   A   She is grateful for the positive attention she receives.

   B   She is relieved to have found people who understand her.

   C   She regrets not having made efforts to meet them sooner.

28   Ruth says that for her, the main disadvantage of having online friends is

   A   not being able to build lasting friendships.

   B   not having physical closeness.

   C   not sharing experiences.

THINK IT THROUGH

You will hear the answers to each question in the same order as you read them. Make sure you read each question and the three options carefully and think about the kind of information you need to listen for.

29 What does Ruth say about getting to know an online friend well?

    A   It is wise not to tell them too much about yourself.

    B   It is useful to find out what their background is.

    C   It is not necessarily important to know them well.

30 What does Ruth think about spending a lot of time with online friends?

    A   It needn't have an impact on social skills.

    B   It results in a lack of good communication skills.

    C   It affects how we interpret people's feelings in real life.

Boost your grade!

1 **Read these recommendations for the Listening Part 4 task. Which one should you not follow?**

    a) Listen to the whole section for each question before selecting your answer.

    b) Underline the key words in each question to help you focus on what you need to listen for.

    c) Listen to the whole test before answering any questions.

    d) Try to predict likely answers before you listen.

2 **Look at question 24 again. Why have these words been underlined? What might you hear Ruth talk about?**

What does Ruth say when asked about online friendships?

    A It's <u>difficult</u> to give proper advice by text.

    B Friends have <u>more</u> contact online than face-to-face.

    C Virtual friendships can be <u>as satisfying as</u> real-life ones.

3a **Work in pairs. Read the questions and options again and underline the words you think will help you to focus on the task.**

3b **Listen to the recording again. Were the words you underlined helpful? If not, why not? Check your answers with the transcript on page 120.**

SPEAKING

Part 1 (2 minutes)

Select one or more questions from any of the following categories, as appropriate.

Holidays

- Where do you like to go on holiday? Why?
- Who do you like to go on holiday with? Why?
- Tell us about a holiday you really enjoyed.
- Do you prefer to go away for a long time, or a short trip? Why?

Special times

- What do you like to do on your birthday? Why?
- Tell us about a special day you've enjoyed with your family recently.
- Are you planning to do anything special this coming weekend? Why / Why not?
- Where do you like to go for a special meal in your town? Why?

Films and television

- Do you prefer to watch films at home or in the cinema? Why?
- What's the best film you've seen recently? Why?
- Do you watch much television in the evenings? Why / Why not?
- Tell us about a good TV programme you enjoy watching.

THINK IT THROUGH

In Part 1 you will be asked personal questions about your likes and dislikes, etc. Remember your answers need to be interesting, but brief.

THINK IT THROUGH

Compare the pictures (don't just describe them) before you answer the question, and try to keep talking for the full minute. The examiner will stop you at the end of the time.

Part 2 (4 minutes)

In this part of the test you are going to have two photographs. You have to talk about your photographs on your own for about a minute, and also answer a question about your partner's photographs.

Candidate A: Here are your photographs. They show **people talking together in different situations.**

Compare the photographs and say **what you think the people are enjoying about talking together in these situations.**

What are the people enjoying about talking together in these situations?

(Candidate B), **do you enjoy chatting to friends? Why?**

Candidate B: Here are your photographs. They show **people listening to music in different situations.**

Compare the photographs and say **why you think the people have decided to listen to music in these situations.**

> **Why have the people decided to listen to music in these situations?**

(Candidate A), **where do you prefer to listen to music? Why?**

Part 3 (4 minutes)

Now, you have to talk about something together for about two minutes.

Some people think it's necessary for everyone to be able to cook well, and other people don't. Here are some things they think about, and a question for you to discuss.

Now, talk to each other about **whether it's important for everyone to learn how to cook**.

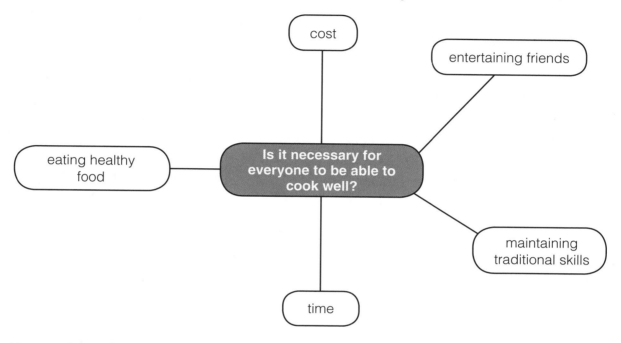

Now you have about a minute to decide **which is the most important reason for everyone to be able to cook**.

 Listen carefully to your partner's answers. You can add to what they say, or disagree with them even if the examiner hasn't asked you the question directly.

Part 4 (4 minutes)

Answer these questions.

- Is it common for young people learn to cook at school in your country? (Why / Why not?)

- Some people choose not to eat meat. Why do you think this is?

- Why do you think programmes about cooking on television are popular?

- Some people say that traditional skills like cooking and sewing are dying out. How do you feel about this? (Why?)

- In many towns there are restaurants with food from different countries. Is this a good thing? (Why?)

- Some people say that the best thing about travelling abroad is trying different food. Do you agree? (Why / Why not?)

How to ... understand text organisation

1 **Work in pairs. Answer the questions.**

a) Do you like travelling to other countries? Why?

b) Have you ever been on an organised trip such as a tour or a cruise? Why / Why not?

c) Do you enjoy travelling with other people? Why / Why not?

d) Would you like to go on a trip to a new country alone? Why / Why not?

Boost your grade!

In Part 6 you have to read a text with six gaps. There are seven possible sentences to fill these gaps. You choose the correct sentence for each gap. You can use each sentence once. You need to think about:

- how the text is organised
- development of ideas through the text
- referents e.g. *this, those*
- linkers e.g. *however*

2a **Work in pairs. Match sentences 1–5 with sentence a–f. Then underline the words in each sentence which helped you complete the task.**

1 I always have a cup of coffee in the morning.

2 I love travelling with friends.

3 You can get information in different ways.

4 It's good to check with travel agents about flights.

5 There's often a tour guide at historical sites.

6 Travel can be expensive.

a) If so, you can ask him or her questions.

b) This means many people choose to stay at home.

c) It helps me wake up.

d) One of these is the internet.

e) They make a trip fun when we're together.

f) They give useful information about them.

2b **Look at the words in sentences a–f that you have underlined. What does each underlined word refer to?**

Example: c) It refers to the cup of coffee.

3 **Work in pairs. Choose the best word to complete each sentence.**

a) I often take photos on holiday as *they* / *that* create good memories.

b) I hate long journeys but to get through *them* / *it* I read books.

c) I discovered the plane was late; *yet* / *this* really annoyed me.

d) I often travel alone, but I don't like *it* / *them* much.

e) Storms can really spoil a holiday when *their* / *they're* unexpected.

f) I'm thinking of going to Spain because *it's* / *its* a place I've never been.

Boost your grade!

Read the complete text through once you have finished the task so you are sure it makes sense.

Checklist for Part 6

Check that:

✓ you have looked for the right referents in each gap

✓ you have filled each gap

✓ you have not used a sentence more than once

✎ Exam task

4   **Work in pairs. Read the sentences A–G. Then mark any referents in each sentence you think might help you to decide where it fits in the text. Now read the whole text.**

You are going to read an article about whether it's better to travel alone or in a group. Six sentences have been removed from the article. Choose from the sentences **A–G** the one which fits each gap (**1–6**). There is one extra sentence which you do not need to use.

Travel – how and why?

People often say that travel broadens the mind, but this opinion is not held by everyone. In fact, quite a large number of people say the opposite! Why is this?

You'd think that visiting different countries would give travellers new experiences that would naturally make them more open-minded. **1** ☐ In this situation people stay together, speaking their own language and only visiting the famous sights. They rarely try to find out more about what real life is like in the country they're visiting. Since such travellers are still having new experiences and seeing the world, they would say that having this group mentality doesn't matter. **2** ☐

When I think back to the first travelling I did outside family holidays, I think of school trips – for example, one year my class went to Paris for a week. The aim of the trip was to practise the language as well as getting to know more about some of the culture on offer. I was about 16, and to be honest I only spoke French about twice during the whole week! The rest of the time I spent with my friends, and although we certainly enjoyed our cultural experiences our language skills remained poor. **3** ☐

When I was older and travelled alone, and had to communicate with everyone en route with no back-up. I had to make my own arrangements and deal with any problems. It taught me so much about myself, and boosted my self-confidence in a surprising way. **4** ☐ That personal development was one bonus of being alone, but I also found myself looking at places with my own eyes. In this way I was getting insights that were not influenced by impressions passed on by people around me. I could make my own judgements and form my own opinions. On a few occasions I joined a tour because that was the easiest and most convenient way to reach far-flung places. **5** ☐ This discovery taught me a great deal about the benefits and drawbacks of different ways of seeing the world.

So to return to the initial question, yes, of course travel broadens the mind, but only if people are open-minded while they do it. It's very easy to pass through a new place without really seeing beneath the surface or appreciating its rich history and culture. Some people are too easily satisfied with taking a selfie in front of an iconic building! **6** ☐ That might sound critical, but those who travel with open minds gain so much more from the experience.

I certainly know how I'll choose to travel in future!

A   Contrast that with my incredibly enriching visit to Asia during a university holiday some years later.

B   I quickly found that I enjoyed these group experiences less than when I was travelling alone.

C   However, I think it does, and I can give examples from my own personal experience to back up my opinion.

D   They then post this on social media in order to boast about their travelling experiences and gain admiration from others.

E   On the other hand, there are so many things to see that tourists are often overwhelmed and can't take it all in.

F   I had neither expected that I could be so independent, nor so capable in these sometimes difficult situations.

G   However, not everyone has this attitude, particularly those who choose to travel in large groups rather than independently.

How to ... write an engaging article

1 **Tick the correct statements about an article.**

An article:

a) is usually written for a magazine, newsletter or website

b) must have a conclusion that summarises the main points

c) should engage and entertain the reader

d) usually uses adjectives and descriptive language

e) can include bullet points

f) should have a title

✏ Exam task

2 **Read the exam task.**

You see this announcement on a musical theatre website.

Articles wanted!

What kind of holiday do you enjoy? How do you decide where to go and what to do on holiday? What's most enjoyable about having a holiday?

The best articles will be published in our next edition of the magazine.

Write your answer in **140–190** words in an appropriate style.

3 **Work in pairs. What should you include in the article? List your ideas.**

4a **Read the three paragraphs and decide which one encourages the reader to continue reading. Match the paragraph to the reason.**

a) I really like holidays and swimming in the sea and I go to the same place every year. I enjoy seeing my friends there.

b) People enjoy different kinds of holidays – relaxing, energetic, cultural – but my favourite is one that combines all three. Let me tell you why.

c) Holidays are great, and there are lots of different types of holiday you can go on. My favourite one is a beach holiday, because it's fun.

1 It speaks directly to the reader.

2 It gives more information about holidays.

3 It uses a lot of different verbs.

> **Boost your grade!**
>
> Make sure you use a wide range of interesting words and speak directly to your reader.

4b **Read the next two paragraphs of the article and choose the phrases which make the sentences more interesting.**

My life is quite **(1)** *all right / boring* – I **(2)** *do the same things / follow the same routine* every day. What I mean is I get up, **(3)** *walk slowly / stroll* to college, study, **(4)** *hang out with / meet* my friends, then go back home. So when I choose a holiday I want to do **(5)** *something nice, / something out of the ordinary* and visit a place where other people don't necessarily go. Because of this I **(6)** *look for / check out* destinations where I can **(7)** *sit / chill out*, but also engage in some physical activities. It would be a bonus if I could also see some unusual sights. That's my ideal scenario because I'm always **(8)** *up for a challenge / interested in new things*.

So what is so enjoyable about having a holiday at all? It seems to me to be the chance to **(9)** *do something different / get out of a rut*, possibly to challenge yourself by trying some **(10)** *extreme / nice* activities or learning a new skill. As you can see, the perfect place for me would be a city with loads of new things to do and experience.

4c **The writer has used different techniques to engage the reader. Highlight these techniques in the paragraphs.**

   a) a rhetorical question

   b) a phrase speaking directly to the reader

   c) an idiom

   d) a phrasal verb

5 **Work in pairs. Choose the best conclusion for the article and give a reason for your choice.**

   a) So that's my ideal holiday, though it may not be everyone's cup of tea. What's yours?

   b) I would really like to go on a holiday like that and hope I will.

   c) I'm planning to have a holiday like that next year.

6 **Work in pairs. Write a title for the article.**

7 **Now write your own answer to the task. Use the checklist to make sure you have made your article as interesting as possible.**

Checklist for Part 2: Article

Have you:

✓ given your article a title?

✓ included at least one rhetorical question?

✓ used interesting language such as phrasal verbs and idioms?

✓ written an amusing or surprising conclusion?

How to ... identify and note down specific information

1 **Work in pairs. Discuss the questions.**

a) Have you ever acted in a stage production? Why / Why not?

b) Do you think being an actor is glamorous? Why / Why not?

c) What do you think is the most difficult thing about being an actor? Why?

d) What do you think would be most enjoyable? Why?

2 **Choose the best word to complete the gaps.**

a) I have always wanted to be an actor – it must be fun / funny!

b) I have never worked / working in the theatre.

c) New actors often employ agents / representatives to help them.

d) I guess actors earn / win a lot of money.

e) Many young actors study performing / performed arts at college.

f) All actors need to do a lot of preparation / prepare.

> ### Boost your grade!
> Before you listen, think about the missing words. Are they verbs, nouns, adjectives or phrases? This will help you to identify the answer as you do the task.

✏ Exam task

3 **Work in pairs. Read the exam task and try and guess the missing words.**

A young actor

You will hear a man called Jack talking to a group of students about being an actor in the theatre. Complete the sentences with a word or short phrase.

Jack became interested in the theatre when he <u>took part in</u> **(1)** .... at college.

It was helping with the **(2)** .... that Jack <u>liked best at first</u>.

Jack did not enjoy the **(3)** .... he had to go to.

According to Jack, it's important for young actors to have a **(4)** .... to encourage them.

Jack's big break came by chance when a **(5)** .... saw him in a television advertisement.

Jack is sure that actors must learn the **(6)** .... as well as their own lines.

Jack uses the word **(7)** .... to describe the discussions between actors before a production.

Jack had not expected professional actors to word so hard at **(8)** ....

Jack felt embarrassed when he had to take a **(9)** .... on stage instead of the correct prop.

Jack uses the word **(10)** .... to describe a good performance in a theatre.

4a Look at the first two sentences in exercise 3 and highlight the words in the transcript below that paraphrase the underlined words.

J: Hi! I'm Jack, and I'm here to talk to you all about being a stage actor. I'm sure you all think it's a glamorous job – well, I'm here to tell you it's far from what you might expect.

My first experience of the theatre came when I was at college – although my main subjects were English and maths, we all had the chance to have a go at performing arts because it was considered to be good for our personal development. That did it for me. In the beginning I got involved in the technical side of back-stage work and I was particularly keen on doing the lighting. I did that on several college productions. Then during rehearsals for one play one of the leading actors dropped out, and I was asked to step in. Once on stage, I was hooked!

4b Now listen and complete the first two sentences in exercise 3.

5 Work in pairs. Underline any words in sentences 3–10 that you think might help you when you listen.

6 Now listen to the rest of the talk and complete sentences 3–10.

7 Work in pairs and check your answers to exercise 6. Use the questions below to help.

Have you

a) got the same answer? If not, why not? Did you misunderstand what was said?

b) written the exact word you heard and not a paraphrase?

c) written a word that is grammatically incorrect?

d) not written an answer at all?

8a Look at the transcript on page 121. Highlight the answers. Did you make any mistakes? Why?

8b Were your original guesses accurate?

> **Boost your grade!**
>
> Use the words before and after the gaps to help you identify the type of word you need for the answer. These words will give you clues about what to listen for – e.g. how the speaker feels, what surprises him, what he thinks is important, etc.

> **Boost your grade!**
>
> Remember that you must complete the sentences with the exact word(s) you hear.

Checklist for Part 2

Check that:

✓ you have not made any spelling mistakes

✓ you have not written too many words

✓ your answer fits into the gap grammatically

✓ you have written the exact word you heard on the recording

How to ... deal with prompts and interact with your partner

1 **Work in pairs. Read the question below.**

> Some people say we watch too much television these days. What do you think?

Think of as many ideas for and against the question as you can, then write them down.

Example: I can learn a lot of things from watching TV programmes, but I can also waste time.

✎ Exam task Part 3

2 **Read the exam task.**

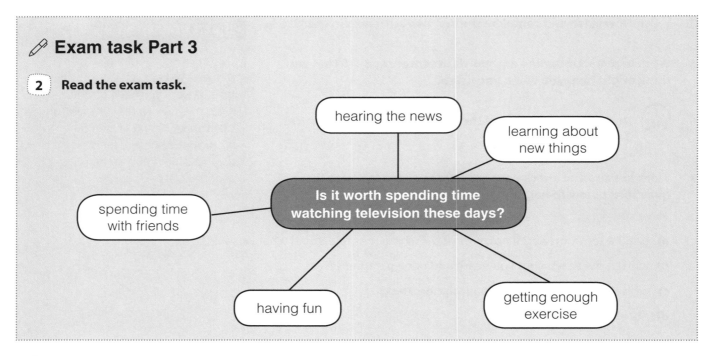

3a **Work in pairs. Look at the notes you made in exercise 1. Do any of them relate to the ideas given in the prompts?**

3b **Think about how each prompt relates to the question and what you could say about each one.**

4 🎧 **Listen to two students discussing the task. Answer the questions.**

   a) Did they mention any of your ideas?

   b) Did they talk about the prompts in order?

   c) Did they talk about all the prompts, or did they leave any out?

   d) Did they add any new ideas of their own?

Boost your grade!

In the actual exam you don't have to talk about all the prompts as you only have two minutes. Try to say as much as you can about each one before moving on to the next.

Listen carefully to what your partner says so that you can respond appropriately.

5 Listen again to the way the students interacted during their discussion. Complete the phrases they used.

a) Let's _____ this one.

b) What do you _____?

c) I know _____ mean.

d) Do you _____ social media?

e) I _____ agree with you.

f) Don't you _____ that …

g) That's _____ true.

h) Let's _____ on.

i) What's your _____ about …?

j) That's a _____ question.

k) But _____ I prefer …

l) I only _____ agree with you

m) In my _____

n) I _____ what you're saying …

o) OK – that's a _____ point,

p) I'm sorry – I still _____ with you.

6a Put the phrases into the correct columns below.

Agreeing	Disagreeing	Asking for opinion	Accepting an opinion	Moving the Conversation on
e				

6b Can you add any more expressions to any column?

7 Work in pairs. Discuss the task yourselves, starting with the prompt the students didn't use. Try to speak for two minutes. Remember to interact with your partner.

8 Now discuss the best reason for not watching too much television. Try to talk for a minute.

READING AND USE OF ENGLISH

Part 1

For questions **1–8**, read the text below and decide which answer (**A**, **B**, **C** or **D**) best fits each gap. There is an example at the beginning **(0)**.

Mark your answers **on the separate answer sheet**.

0   **A** added   **B** put   **C** increased   **D** supplemented

0	A	B	C	D
	▄▄	☐	☐	☐

I hate cabbage

Were you a fussy eater when you were a child? Did you throw a tantrum whenever your mother

(0) .... green vegetables to your plate? Perhaps your parents refused to **(1)** ....

you leave the table until you'd eaten everything? Most of us have **(2)** .... memories. But why

do we have these food fads, and why are so many children **(3)** .... to try new foods?

For years people have assumed it was the parents' fault.

New research suggests parents are not to blame – **(4)** .... it's all down to our genes (rather

like nearly everything **(5)** ....)! It appears that we dislike certain foods and are unwilling to

try others simply because we are born with this **(6)** .... and these genes influence our eating

from the very beginning. Parents can still help however, but not by **(7)** .... food on a child –

that is likely to do more harm than good. Encouragement and understanding will help if the parents

can **(8)** ....

1	**A** allow	**B** permit	**C** let	**D** accept
2	**A** same	**B** like	**C** related	**D** similar
3	**A** anxious	**B** reluctant	**C** insecure	**D** careful
4	**A** apparently	**B** obviously	**C** knowingly	**D** subconsciously
5	**A** more	**B** besides	**C** also	**D** else
6	**A** desire	**B** feeling	**C** tendency	**D** trend
7	**A** making	**B** obliging	**C** insisting	**D** forcing
8	**A** continue	**B** keep	**C** persevere	**D** repeat

THINK IT THROUGH

Don't look at the options before reading the text. The correct word may come to you instinctively as you read.

Part 2

For questions **9–16**, read the text below and think of the word which best fits each gap. Use only one word in each gap. There is an example at the beginning **(0)**.

Write your answers **IN CAPITAL LETTERS on the separate answer sheet**.

Example: | **0** | T | O | | | | | | | | | | | | | |

Buying something? Take a selfie.

Since technology first allowed us **(0)** .... buy things without cash there have been people ready to use technology to steal our money. Credit cards can **(9)** .... stolen, PIN numbers copied, online bank accounts attacked **(10)** .... hackers. The experts are fighting a continual battle to stay one step ahead, and **(11)** .... of the latest security ideas is the selfie! Soon, it seems, we shall be able to take a selfie to prove **(12)** .... identity when we buy something online or at a checkout. The photo can't be used by someone else as the app requires **(13)** .... person who is taking the selfie to blink, shut their eyes, to show **(14)** .... it is a live photo! Biometric security – eye scans, fingerprints and face photography – will inevitably become commonplace and **(15)** .... most people it will be far easier to take a selfie **(16)** .... than remember a PIN number or password. Yet, how long will this be safe?

> Read the whole sentence again and think about the structure – is it active or passive?

> Think about whether the gap is part of a comparative structure.

Part 3

For questions **17–24**, read the text below. Use the word given in capitals at the end of some of the lines to form a word that fits in the gap in the same line. There is an example at the beginning **(0)**.

Write your answers **IN CAPITAL LETTERS on the separate answer sheet**.

Example:

0	D	E	C	O	R	A	T	I	O	N						

No, you can't work here!

Tattooing dates back thousands of years as a form of **(0)** ....,   **DECORATE**

tribal symbolism and identification. It has even been used to provide

(17) .... information such as blood type. However, the   **MEDICINE**

current **(18)** .... started in the last century and today   **FASCINATE**

there are numerous licensed tattoo parlours. Tattoos once considered

ugly are now thought **(19)** .... and copied by people   **TREND**

ranging from teenagers to **(20)** .... One reason for this   **PENSION**

popularity has been the number of celebrities who openly display

their body art. Tattooing has finally become **(21)** ....   **RESPECT**

(22) ...., there have been some problems for people with   **INEVITABLE**

visible body art when looking for **(23)** .... But recent   **EMPLOY**

statistics show that the attitude of employers to tattoos is changing.

40% of people in the UK now have a tattoo and more jobs are open

to them, including the police force. The argument against employees

with tattoos will soon become as **(24)** .... as the one   **RELEVANT**

against women wearing trousers to work!

THINK IT THROUGH

When you change a word, think carefully about the spelling,
e.g. In example (0), the verb 'decorate' ends in '-e' but the
noun form 'decoration' has no '-e'

Part 4

For questions **25–30**, complete the second sentence so that it has a similar meaning to the first sentence, using the word given. **Do not change the word given.** You must use between **two** and **five** words including the word given. Here is an example **(0)**.

Example:

0 It's fine for students to eat in the classrooms at lunchtime.

ALLOWED

Students ....*are allowed to*............... eat in the classrooms at lunchtime.

---

25 The test was so difficult that I couldn't finish it.

SUCH

It was .... that I couldn't finish it.

26 'Helen, do you know where your brother is?' asked Angela. ○················

Angela asked Helen ....
brother was.

> Think about both the tense and pronouns here.

IF

27 I first met Brian three years ago. ○················

KNOWN

I .... three years.

> Think about both the tense and the time expression here.

28 Let's not watch TV, but listen to some music.

INSTEAD

Let's listen to .... TV.

29 I didn't go out because I didn't have any money.

HAD

If I .... money, I would have gone out.

30 I have never eaten in this restaurant before.

TIME

This is .... ever eaten in this restaurant.

THINK IT THROUGH

Sometimes there are two things you need to be careful about when rewriting.

Part 5

You are going to read part of a story in which a young girl talks about a competition. For questions **31–36** choose the answer (**A**, **B**, **C** or **D**) which you think fits best according to the text.

Mark your answers **on the separate answer sheet**.

Going home

It was approaching six o'clock as I drove up the hill leading to Steysbridge. I'd been listening to the news on the radio and reflecting on how depressing the items seemed to be these days; muggings, robberies, war, murders. I was completely unprepared for the blast of evening sunlight that hit me as I reached the top of the hill. It blinded me for a second until my eyes adjusted. How could I have forgotten the amazing sunsets that I had experienced so often as a teenager, driving back from university for those precious holiday weeks at home? They were always anticipated then. I would look forward to cresting the top of the hill and seeing the incredible cloud formations that were so often edged with gold as the sun sank. I felt a sudden sadness that life had moved on and blotted out those memories.

This homecoming was going to be very different to those carefree student ones. People would be missing. The neighbours who had given me sweets and cakes after school while my parents were still at work had both died a decade previously, followed by my mother a couple of years later. Now my father lived there alone, becoming bitter in his old age at a world which had taken his wife and not him. We had not spoken since her funeral. Marrying an American and raising a family a thousand miles away had angered him. He had always been an angry man, my father. He had cut off communication with me as had the ocean that physically separated us.

It was as I descended the hill, a little recklessly despite the steepness of the slope, that I saw the smoke rising, a grey column drifting straight up towards the clouds, close to the rising spire of the church. I initially thought it must have been a garden bonfire. It was November after all and people in the area often used to burn garden waste in the late afternoon. I could still bring back the lovely smell of wood smoke which, wherever I went in the world would always conjure up autumn in my home town. But the smoke this evening had a darkness to it and something told me it was not garden waste that was being burned.

Before my mind reached the more obvious conclusion, blue lights flashed in my rear view mirror and the sing song siren of a fire engine did my thinking for me. Automatically I steered towards the grass verge and the truck hurtled past me faster than it should have done considering the incline, but I imagined with a far smarter driver than me behind the wheel. I watched it veer right at the bottom of the hill and disappear into the group of buildings that made up the village. The siren was fading, although I could still see flashes of the blue light as it passed the spaces between houses. For some reason I expected it to turn up into market street but it didn't. It went down towards the river and stopped, just before the bridge, lights blazing, at a point I was only too familiar with. I knew without being able to see directly that it was the lane leading to my father's house. Suddenly the dark smoke enveloped the blue lights and there was a red glow inside the cloud. It wasn't a reflection of the sunset. My heart beat started racing and I instinctively reached for the bottle of tablets on the passenger seat. A sleepy voice came from the back of the car: 'Why have we stopped mummy? Are we there yet?' my daughter asked. 'Can I see grandad now?'

31   Why did the brightness of the sun surprise the writer?

   A   she hadn't realised the time of day

   B   she wasn't wearing the right glasses

   C   she hadn't used this road very often before

   D   she'd been thinking about something else

32   How did the sight of the sunset affect the writer?

   A   she was surprised by its beauty

   B   she was reminded that life had changed

   C   she was excited by what was going to happen

   D   she felt let down by her memories

33   What does the writer imply about her father?

   A   he had chosen a lonely life

   B   he resented her success

   C   he was opposed to her marriage

   D   he had poor communication skills

34   In paragraph 3 the writer makes a wrong assumption about the smoke because of

   A   the time of year.

   B   the location.

   C   her position on the road.

   D   the colour.

35   The appearance of the fire engine made her

   A   angry because of its speed.

   B   aware of how badly she was driving.

   C   realise something serious was happening.

   D   stop thinking about the fire.

36   What do we learn about the writer in the final paragraph?

   A   she may have a problem with anxiety

   B   she is afraid for her daughter

   C   she doesn't want to restart the car

   D   she does things without thinking

THINK IT THROUGH

A good way to check if you have chosen the correct option is to ask yourself why the other three options are NOT correct.

Part 6

You are going to read an article about health choices. Six sentences have been removed from the article. Choose from the sentences **A–G** the one which fits each gap (**37–42**). There is one extra sentence you do not need to use.

Mark your answers **on the separate answer sheet**.

A healthier you

You already know the basics – apples are better for you than doughnuts, and exercise is something you *should* do. But sometimes the right health choices aren't as obvious.

You may think watching a film is an efficient way to unwind while you have a post working day snack; after all, once you refuel, there's a lot to do. **37** ⬚ In fact, one study found that people ate 71 percent more macaroni and cheese when watching TV. Why? Instead of stopping when they're full, distracted eaters rely on external cues, like the end of a TV programme, to stop a snack session, says eating behaviour expert Brian Wansink, author of *Mindless Eating*.

One answer is to measure out a single serving of a snack before you sit down. **38** ⬚ It can take your stomach up to 20 minutes to let your brain know it's full.

Another problem can be when dinner feels like an eternity away and you pick up a granola bar or a fruit smoothie to stop a growling stomach. However, you're soon hungry again. Why? **39** ⬚ (Some granola bars contain as much of it as chocolate bars.) Sweet treats trigger your body to release a flood of insulin, a hormone that causes your blood sugar to plummet, according to Jo Bartell, a registered dietician. When that happens, the hunger returns, your energy nose-dives – and focusing on anything active, physically or mentally, seems impossible.

Reading labels is your best weapon against stealth sugar sources that can cause a system crash. (Your intake should max out at 20 to 32 grams a day, says the American Heart Association, so budget accordingly.) **40** ⬚ Watch out for them and steer away from those red lights.

There's another bad habit we often fall into. Whether it's a question of not having enough time or trying to lose weight quickly, but many people skip breakfast. This is NOT a good idea. **41** ⬚ Protein gives a morning meal staying power, so pair toast with an egg. In addition to having a decent breakfast getting enough sleep, roughly eight hours, will help you stay alert throughout the day, feel less anxious and even help you make healthier choices.

It's understandable. **42** ⬚ But when you eat a lunch that's practically 100 percent simple carbohydrates, you're missing out on the nutrients that help keep you active and your concentration focused all the way through the day: fibre (found in fruits and veggies), protein (which you get from lean meat, like turkey or chicken, and from fish and beans), and healthy fats (think avocado or peanut butter).

To stay full, energized and healthy, practise the three-for-three rule: Eat three meals a day that each have a mix of all three nutrients. A sandwich made with turkey (protein – check!) on whole wheat bread (to get those high-fibre carbs) with avocado (yes – healthy fat!) is definitely a winning lunch. It makes a lot of sense and your body and mind will thank you.

A And prior to getting seconds, pause for a quick timeout.

B Many tins and packets carry traffic light type symbols to indicate how healthy or not a particular food is.

C The problem is, your hand hits the bottom of the chip bag faster when you're multitasking, which can leave you feeling full up and lethargic.

D These people have a tougher time remembering things and feel fatigued in the afternoon.

E Many of those 'healthy' choices are actually loaded with sugar.

F Or instead of having two slices of pizza, take one, then pair it with sliced vegetables and fruit to balance things out.

G Sometimes the cafeteria's healthier meal options with vegetables don't entice you quite like the crisps or chips.

Boost your grade!

Look at the reference words to help you choose the correct options.

What do the following reference words refer to?

a) line 23 'it' ....

b) line 35 'them' ....

c) option D 'these people' ....

d) option E 'those healthy choices' ....

Part 7

You are going read a weekly TV review about documentaries. For questions **43–52** choose from the sections (**A–D**). The sections may be chosen more than once.

Mark your answers **on the separate answer sheet**.

In which paragraph does the writer

speculate on something that might affect **all of us**? 43 [ ] ◦····

> Find a word that means 'all of us' not only a small group.

comment on a programme that holds the viewers' interest from the start? 44 [ ]

review a programme that has been seen before? 45 [ ]

describe something that experts disagree about? 46 [ ]

outline a story that compares different ways the same animal has been treated? 47 [ ]

imply that information needs to be acted on **soon**? 48 [ ] ◦····

> Find a word or phrase which implies that quick action is needed.

talk about exploiting information learned from another experience? 49 [ ]

mention how an animal has been tricked? 50 [ ]

add to some information that we already share? 51 [ ]

····◦ describe **measures** being taken to protect a species? 52 [ ]

> Find a text which lists a number of different ways people are trying to help.

A great week for wildlife documentaries

A First up on Monday evening was a fascinating programme, repeated from last autumn's *Natural Festival* series, about how farmers in Africa have managed to solve a problem with the local elephant population. These days we're used to hearing horrific stories about the damage man has done to these animals, but this story focused on how man can co-exist with elephants without harming them. Farmers grow crops which elephants like to eat and so constantly knock down any barriers the farmers try to put up to keep them out. The elephants are intelligent and even work out how to get through or deactivate electric fencing. The answer was reached through the old story about elephants being scared of small things, like mice. It's not the tiny creature they are frightened of – it's the surprise factor. Farmers realised that they could use swarms of bees to help protect their boundaries. The elephants are known to run from hives in the trees when angry bees circle their heads. Farmers are now placing hives around their fences, linked by wires. When the elephants disturb the wires, the bees swarm angrily and they run away! The farmers can also sell the honey – a win-win situation.

B To continue with the bee theme, there was another, quite different programme about them this week, this time on Channel 15, which was really thought-provoking. It's common knowledge that there are serious problems with the honey bee populations. Without bees, flowers, fruits and crops would be affected by reduced pollination. According to Einstein – if bees totally disappeared from our planet, humans would not be able to survive for longer than four years! Unfortunately, for a long time now the numbers of honey bees have been in decline and according to scientists there are several possible reasons for this. The bees may have been affected by environmental changes or pesticides could be to blame, in particular the use of neoncontinoids.

C This latter documentary focused on how these pesticides have divided scientific opinion and it was really quite scary. Scientists have suspected that neoncontinoids are harming the bees but tests have shown nothing wrong in those insects that have been exposed to them. However, other research indicates that the insecticide doesn't kill immediately but causes brain damage – affecting the bees' memories for smell and direction. This means that they cannot find food and they cannot get back to their hives. In time the bee colonies die out. The documentary concluded that the situation is fast becoming an emergency. If you missed it, it's definitely worth watching on catch up.

D Moving on from bees, my final choice of documentary this week is the latest in the series about endangered seabirds. It opened with the unlikely shot of baby albatross chicks sitting on flower pots! An attention grabbing opener if ever I saw one. Apparently one particular albatross species, the Chatham albatross, only breeds in one place in the world, an island called The Pyramid in the Chatham Islands. Albatross always return to the place they were born to raise their own families so if something catastrophic happened to the site on this island the whole species could die out. Therefore albatross chicks are being translocated to another island to grow up and encouraged to believe that this new island is 'home'. With luck they will return there to breed and ensure that there are two nesting sites in the world. And the flower pots? Albatross build pillars of mud for nests and the chicks sit on top of them as they grow. The flower pots do the job just as well!

WRITING

Part 1

You **must** answer this question. Write your answer in **140–190** words in an appropriate style on the separate answer sheet.

1   In your English class you have been talking about whether reading newspapers is the best way to find out about the news. Now, your English teacher has asked you to write an essay.

Write your essay using **all** the notes and giving reasons for your point of view.

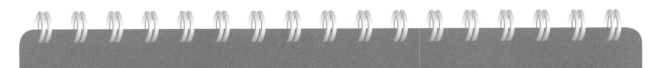

Many people think that reading newspapers is the best way to find out about the news. Do you agree?

Notes

Write about:

1. keeping up to date

2. forming opinions

3. .... (your own idea)

THINK IT THROUGH

Spend an equal amount of time on each question as they carry the same marks. Don't spend more time on Part 1.

Part 2

Write an answer to one of the questions **2–4** in this part. Write your answer in **140–190** words in an appropriate style on the separate answer sheet. Put the question number in the box at the top of the answer sheet.

---

2   You see this announcement on a musical theatre website.

> **Reviews wanted**
>
> We want some reviews of musicals that are based on a book or a story. We want to know something about the book, and how similar the musical is. Say whether you thought the book or musical was best, and whether you recommend the musical and why.
>
> The best reviews will be posted on our website.

Write your **review**.

3   You see this advertisement in an English-language magazine.

> **Volunteer with us for two weeks this July!**
>
> Are you aged 16–18? Why not volunteer to help us with our summer school programme?
>
> We need people who enjoy organising fun activities for children, and who want to experience life in another country. We provide accommodation and meals.
>
> Send a letter to Sue Robbins, saying why you would like to volunteer with us, and what you are good at.
>
> Please let us know what your standard of English is, and whether you have any questions about the programme.

Write your **letter**.

THINK IT THROUGH

Letter: This letter is formal in style. Remember to include all the information and include at least one question to ask about the programme.

4

> Your local council is considering opening a new sports facility in the area, and wants local residents to give their opinions by sending in a report.
>
> Your report should:
>
> - Include information about current facilities
> - Explain why you need a new facility
> - Recommend the new facility you would like to have, with reasons

Write your **report**.

LISTENING

Part 1

 You will hear people talking in eight different situations. For questions **1–8**, choose the best answer (**A**, **B**, or **C**).

1 You hear a boy talking about his ambition.
Why does he want to be a scientist?

  A   to make improvements to others' lives

  B   to get other people interested in the subject

  C   to research topics he has learned about at school

2 You hear two friends talking about painting pictures.
What do they both say about it?

  A   They would like to improve their techniques.

  B   It makes problems seem less important.

  C   It makes them feel relaxed afterwards.

3 You hear an announcement at a sports event. O
What is the man doing?

  A   giving a warning

  B   offering some advice

  C   making an enquiry

> Some questions ask you to sum up the purpose of what the speaker says. Listen for examples of language that are used in particular situations. Imperatives may be used for warning, e.g. 'Be careful!' or 'Don't go near ...'; 'you should (not)' or 'If I were you' are common ways of giving advice; 'Could ...?' is often used in polite requests for making enquiries.

4 You hear two friends talking about skateboarding.
How does the girl feel?

  A   nervous about a skateboarding competition

  B   disappointed with local skateboarding facilities

  C   amazed by her friend's new skateboarding skills

> ### THINK IT THROUGH
>
> Underline key words in the questions and options. This will help you focus on the information you need to listen for.

PHOTOCOPIABLE

5   You hear two friends talking about a book they have read.
          What does the girl think about it?

    A   Its ending didn't live up to expectations.

    B   Its main character was unrealistic.

    C   Its written style was uninteresting.

6   You hear a girl talking about a website she has used.
          What does she say about it?

    A   It was easy to use.

    B   It was helpful for her studies.

    C   It had some interesting activities.

7   You hear two friends talking about a song they have heard.
          What do both speakers think about it?

    A   the lyrics are interesting

    B   the music is memorable

    C   the singer's voice is good

8   You hear two ballet dancers talking about training.
          What do they agree about?

    A   how well-prepared they are for a performance

    B   how physically tiring their work schedule is

    C   how inspiring their director is

THINK IT THROUGH

If you aren't sure of an answer, don't worry. Keep listening.
You can check again when you listen the second time.

Part 2

 You will hear a girl called Joanna talking about a volunteering project she has been involved in.

For questions **9–18**, complete the sentences with a word or short phrase.

Volunteering: teaching English in India

Joanna was pleased to get a **(9)** .... meal on the plane to India.

When Joanna arrived in India, she experienced feelings of **(10)** ....

The kind of area Joanna had asked to be sent to was **(11)** ....

Joanna enjoyed seeing **(12)** .... in the street as she travelled by bus to her destination.

Joanna describes the difference in ability between the students she had to teach as **(13)** ....

Initially, Joanna decided to work on **(14)** .... skills in English with the students.

Joanna made sure she included **(15)** .... in her classes, which she knew students would like.

When she realised how much progress her students had made, Joanna experienced a feeling of

(16) ....

In her free time, Joanna acquired skills in **(17)** .... with the family she stayed with.

At the end of her stay the volunteers held a party, where they taught English **(18)** .... to the guests.

 THINK IT THROUGH

The sentences always follow the same order as the recording.

Part 3

 You will hear five short extracts in which people are talking about celebrations they helped to organise. For questions **19–23**, choose from the list (**A–H**) how each speaker says they felt about the celebration. Use the letters only once. There are three extra letters which you do not need to use.

A   relieved that it had gone well

B   delighted to see family members

C   pleased about some of the activities

D   surprised that so many people came

E   proud of what they achieved in advance

F   enthusiastic about repeating the experience

G   impressed by some news that was announced

H   grateful to have received help when preparing

Speaker 1	19
Speaker 2	20
Speaker 3	21
Speaker 4	22
Speaker 5	23

THINK IT THROUGH

A speaker might express feelings about various things in the options as they speak. Make sure the option you choose answers the question in this case how the speakers felt about the **celebration**.

Write your answer during the first listening and check it when you listen again. It doesn't matter if you make notes or cross out answers on the question paper as you will transfer your answers onto an answer sheet at the end of the test.

Part 4

 You will hear part of an interview with a psychologist called Mark Bradshaw, who is talking about how to give up bad habits.

For questions **24–30**, choose the best answer (**A**, **B**, or **C**).

THINK IT THROUGH

Don't worry if you lose your place as you listen. The questions will help you to find your place again, so just keep listening.

24   What reason does Mark give for people missing breakfast?

    A   being lazy

    B   being too tired

    C   being in a hurry

> Think of synonyms for 'lazy', 'tired' and 'be in a hurry'. Mark uses synonyms for all three in the interview. Why are two answers incorrect? Check your answers in the transcript on page 124.

25   Mark believes people should tell others about their intention to give up a habit so that they

    A   feel more determined to carry it out.

    B   can receive help in deciding what to do.

    C   gain the support needed to implement the plans.

26   When Mark kept a record of his snack-eating habit he felt

    A   ashamed of the way he had been acting.

    B   amazed to discover the reasons behind it.

    C   annoyed with himself for not doing it sooner.

27   Mark says that when a bad habit has been formed,

    A   it can be harder than people think to give up.

    B   it requires a lot of concentration to stop doing it.

    C   it is crucial to avoid situations which cause it to happen.

Mark mentions 'a barrier'. Which answer is this similar to?

○ **28** What is Mark's definition of what he calls 'creating obstacles'?

    A requesting that people speak up when poor behaviour begins

    B making it physically difficult to participate in bad habits

    C trying to distract attention by doing a physical activity

29 Mark recognised that he bit his fingernails when he felt

    A nervous about something he was about to do.

    B annoyed by something someone was saying.

    C bored with an activity he was engaged in.

Mark uses synonyms for 'nervous', 'annoyed' and 'bored' in the interview. What are they? Why are two answers not correct? Check your answers in the transcript on page 124.

○ **30** What does Mark recommend to someone who drinks a lot of cola?

    A talking to themselves to break the habit

    B rewarding themselves for good behaviour

    C thinking of long-term goals as a discouragement

Mark mentions 'a motivator'. Which answer is this similar to?

SPEAKING

Part 1 (2 minutes)

Select one or more questions from any of the following categories, as appropriate.

Music

- Would you like to play a musical instrument? (Why?)
- Who do you like to listen to music with? (Why?)
- Do you often go to live concerts? (Why / Why not?)
- What's your favourite kind of music? (Why?)

Getting around

- Do you use public transport much where you live? (Why / Why not?)
- How do you prefer to travel on long journeys – car or bus? (Why?)
- What do you usually do when you're on a long journey? (Why?)
- Do you often cycle to different places? (Why / Why not?)

Work and study

- Do you use the internet when you are studying? (Why / Why not?)
- What kind of work would you like to do in the future? (Why?)
- Do you prefer to study alone, or with friends? (Why?)
- Is there anything new that you would like to learn? (Why / Why not?)

THINK IT THROUGH

Don't respond to your partner in this part – you only need to answer questions about yourself.

Part 2 (4 minutes)

In this part of the test you are going to have two photographs. You have to talk about your photographs on your own for about a minute, and also answer a question about your partner's photographs.

Candidate A: Here are your photographs They show **people using mobile phones in different situations**.

Compare the photographs and say **why you think the people are using mobile phones in these situations**.

Why are the people using mobile phones in these situations?

(Candidate B), **do you use your phone to take photographs? (Why / Why not?)**

THINK IT THROUGH

Try to organise your talk using linking words such as 'whereas' and 'on the other hand' so that your ideas are easy to follow.

Candidate B: Here are your photographs. They show **people eating lunch in different places**.

Compare the photographs and say **why you think the people have decided to eat lunch in these places**.

> **Why have the people decided to eat lunch in these places?**

(Candidate A), **which of these places would you prefer to eat lunch in? (Why?)**

Part 3 (4 minutes)

Now, you have to talk about something together for about two minutes.

Some people think young people should take part in team sports. Here are some things they think about, and a question for you to discuss.

Now talk to each other about **whether it's a good idea for young people to take part in team sports**.

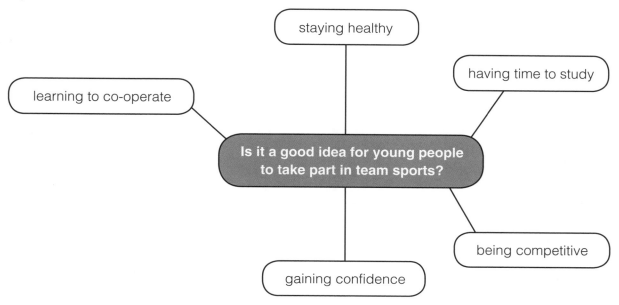

staying healthy

having time to study

learning to co-operate

Is it a good idea for young people to take part in team sports?

being competitive

gaining confidence

Now you have about a minute to decide **which one is the best reason for encouraging young people to take part in team sports**.

You don't have to discuss ALL the prompts and you don't have to reach a decision.

Part 4 (4 minutes)

Answer these questions.

• What's the most popular team sport in your country? (Why?)

• Are there many opportunities for taking part in team sports where you live? (Why / Why not?)

• Why do you think some people prefer to do individual sports instead of team sports?

• Do you think that there is too much sport shown on television? (Why / Why not?)

• Some people say that sports people make good role models. What do you think?

• Are international sporting events such as the Football World Cup a good thing? (Why / Why not?)

How to ... find information in different texts

1 **Scan texts A–E quickly. What are they about?**

a) people's attitude towards their work

b) the advantages of having a good job

c) interesting careers for people to follow

2 **Read text A and answer questions 1–3. Underline the parts of the text where you found each answer.**

Where does the writer mention

a change in perspective on her own position? **1** ☐

an admission that she dislikes some aspects of her work? **2** ☐

an awareness that some things take a long time? **3** ☐

Boost your grade!

In Part 7 you have to read one long text divided into sections, or several short texts. There are ten questions and you have to identify the correct text or section of text that answers each question. You can choose the same section to answer more than one question. You need to

- read quickly to locate information
- think about paraphrasing of words in the questions and texts
- identify the attitude and opinion of the writer

A

I've loved working in the newspaper office – everyone's so friendly. The workload itself isn't overly stressful, although sometimes it can seem a bit repetitive – particularly as I'm not keen on doing some of the more mundane tasks! I always thought I'd work there for ages, but actually I've now come to realise that it could be rather limiting – that's made me consider other options and I can see that I could make more of my skills. I've started applying for things outside my comfort zone; I've had a couple of unsuccessful interviews, and though I don't like it I've accepted that change is certainly not going to happen in the next couple of days! In the meantime I'm going to relax and be confident that things will work out.

3 **Look at the parts of the text you have underlined.**

Which one

a) is a paraphrase of the main idea?

b) uses a phrase that introduces the writer's opinion?

c) uses a phrase that shows the writer understands something new?

Boost your grade!

Don't read all the texts in detail - you won't have time. Read the questions, then scan each text looking for the information you need.

✏ Exam task

4 **You are going to read four texts about people and work. For questions 4–10, choose from the texts B–E. The texts may be chosen more than once.**

In which text does the writer mention

a feeling of insecurity in the workplace	**4** ☐
an acceptance of a lack of ability	**5** ☐
finding the work very satisfying	**6** ☐
an unexpected benefit of a subject studied	**7** ☐
a problem that was difficult to solve	**8** ☐
the advantage of the hours worked	**9** ☐
a comparison with previous jobs	**10** ☐

B

I always did well at school and so when I started work in an office it came as a bit of a shock to find that I wasn't as good as other people – I lost a lot of confidence at first. I think that it really brought it home to me when I was asked to deal with a particularly difficult situation with a client, and I just didn't know what the answer was or what to do. I learned a lot from that though, and things are much better now. I have great friends in the office, and we spend a lot of time together – I guess I'll stay there for a long time.

C

I always knew I wanted to work with animals, and although I had to study for a long time I now work as a vet. I'm lucky because I don't have a difficult boss and I love what I do – I feel great when I can make a sick animal better. When I was studying I did lots of part-time jobs but that was just to earn money – they were nothing like what I do now. My ambition is to have my own practice, and then I can do what I want without having to report to anyone.

D

I'm really into sport, and it was a no-brainer that I'd work in something connected with that. Unfortunately I was never much good at sport myself, so helping other people who were better than me was the next best thing. I'm now a physiotherapist, and although I sometimes feel a bit disappointed that I'm not a top sportsperson I get more pleasure from what I do than I'd ever expected.

E

My parents always wanted me to be a teacher, but I wasn't keen. I did lots of different jobs, nothing special, and then decided to go to college to do Spanish. I hadn't realised how easy I would find it, nor how easy it would make travelling – that's now become my main hobby. Unfortunately I still had to work, and I kind of fell into teaching but now I really enjoy it. Because I love travelling, the long holidays are a real bonus and so I feel I have the best of both worlds.

Checklist for Part 7

Check that:

✓ you have not chosen a text because the word in the option is the same as the word in the text (a wordspot)

✓ you have an answer for every question

80 mins

How to ... present your ideas appropriately

1 Tick the one statement about reports that is **not** true.

A report should:

a) use semi-formal language

b) make suggestions or recommendations

c) include headings and bullet points

d) entertain the reader

e) provide information

✏ Exam task

2 Read the exam task.

> Your town is thinking of holding an environmental day, and wants everyone to become involved in some activities to help improve the town. You have been asked to write a report. In your report you should:
>
> • explain the aim of the report
>
> • suggest some activities that could be included in the day
>
> • say whether you recommend holding the day

3a The writer has decided to use three headings for the report. Which one should **not** be used?

a) Introduction

b) Reasons why people want to improve the town

c) Suggestions for activities

d) Recommendations

3b Complete the table in exercise 4 with these ideas and the headings from exercise 3a.
You do not need to use all the sentences and headings.

a) There is a lot of litter in the town.

b) There could be a quiz about the environment in the evening with prizes.

c) The aim of the report is to say whether the day would be a good idea and suggest activities that could take place.

d) People don't take environmental problems seriously and need to know more.

e) People who live in the town could work in teams to pick up litter.

f) The landfill site is too big and people need to know more about recycling.

g) A day like this is a good idea because it brings people together and creates a town community.

h) Posters could be put around the town to explain more about recycling.

4 **Work in pairs. Can you add any more ideas of your own to the table?**

Introduction		
	There could be a quiz about the environment in the evening with prizes.	

5 **Read the phrases below. Which one is not used to make a recommendation?**

a) I think it would be good to …

b) In my opinion we should …

c) I feel it could be useful if we …

d) I think we have to …

e) I strongly recommend …

> **Boost your grade!**
>
> Remember to include reasons for the suggestions you make. Use bullet points.

6 **Work in pairs. Complete the suggestions.**

a) People who live in the town could work in teams to pick up litter, because ....
....

b) Posters could be put up around the town to explain more about recycling, because ....
....

c) There could be a quiz about the environment in the evening with prizes because ....
....

7 **Read the task below. Write your own report, using headings and bullet points.**

> Your local college wants to start an English language club for the students so that they can practise speaking in English. The Principal of the college has asked you to write a report.
> In your report you should:
>
> - explain the aim of the report
>
> - suggest some activities the English language club could do
>
> - say whether you recommend starting the club

Write your answer in **140–190** words in an appropriate style.

Checklist for Part 2: Reports

Have you:

✓ included all the information required?

✓ made appropriate recommendations and suggestions with reasons?

✓ used bullet points and headings?

✓ divided your ideas into clear sections?

> **Boost your grade!**
>
> Make sure you present your ideas clearly so that the reader can find all the information they need easily.

How to ... identify attitude and feelings

1 **Work in pairs. Discuss the questions.**

a) Do you like sports? Why / Why not?

b) Do you prefer to watch sport or play it? Why?

c) Is there a sport you think you'd be good at? What is it? Why?

d) How easy do you think it is to become really good at a particular sport? Why?

e) Why do you think some people dedicate themselves to becoming good at sport?

f) How do you think it would feel to win a gold medal?

g) What do you think about the money successful sportspeople make? Why?

2 **Work in pairs. How does the speaker feel? Match the words in the box with the sentences.**

> amused   disappointed   grateful   honoured   hopeful
> impressed   keen   motivated   nervous   relieved

a) I really appreciated their help.   *grateful*

b) That interview really made me laugh, it was so funny!

c) The match was a real let-down – I expected a better game.

d) I'd really love to come with you!

e) That player is fantastic, I've never seen anyone as good.

f) I'm not sure if I can do it – I feel quite scared.

g) I didn't expect to be elected – I feel very proud.

h) I think I can win the game – I have a good chance.

i) I'm determined to win – to please my family.

j) I'm glad I worked so hard – all the effort was worth it.

3a **Work in pairs. Choose the best meaning for the underlined word or phrase.**

1 I wanted to <u>take up</u> tennis. *a*   a) start   b) give up

2 It was <u>a highlight</u>   a) a difficult moment   b) a good moment

3 I like to <u>make a commitment</u>   a) accept a decision   b) be dedicated to something

4 Being successful brings <u>recognition</u>   a) fame   b) understanding

5 I loved it from <u>the word go</u>   a) the beginning   b) time to time

6 I took it all <u>in my stride</u>   a) it made me nervous   b) it didn't worry me

3b **Do the expressions in exercise 3a show a positive or negative attitude?**

4 Work in pairs. The phrases 1–8 describe how a person felt after winning a sports competition. Match them to the actual words spoken a–h.

1 relieved to have done enough preparation

2 pleased the family were watching

3 honoured to have taken part in the competition

4 very surprised to have been so successful

5 excited about future opportunities

6 proud of the achievement

7 motivated to work harder

8 hopeful of similar success in other sports

a) '… made me more determined to do my best to improve.'

b) 'It was special to be in the event.'

c) '… but glad that I'd worked so hard.'

d) 'Having my family there was the real icing on the cake.'

e) 'I couldn't have been more delighted with what I'd managed to do.'

f) 'If only I could do as well in other sports.'

g) 'I was totally amazed by how well I'd done.'

h) 'This was just the start, and it was so thrilling.'

Exam task

5 You will hear five short extracts in which people are talking about winning their first medal in a sports competition. Listen and tick the phrases you hear from phrases a–h in exercise 4.

6 Now listen again. Choose from sentences 1–8 how each person felt after winning their medal.

7 Work in pairs. Read the transcript on pages 124–125 and underline the parts where you found the answers.

Checklist for Part 3

Check that:

✓ you haven't used a letter more than once

✓ you have put the letters in the right place

40 mins

How to ... answer the question and engage in a discussion

1 Work in pairs. Look at the questions (1–5) a student asked about Part 4 and match them to the answers (a–e).

1 In Part 4 do I have to speak on my own?

2 Am I marked on what I say, or the way I say it?

3 How long should my answers be?

4 What happens if I can't think of anything to say?

5 What is the difference between the questions the examiner asks in Part 1 and in Part 4?

a) You can say this, or you can ask your partner what they think. You won't lose marks if you can't think of an answer to one question.

b) It's a language exam, so although what you say has to be relevant and needs to answer the question, you are not judged on your opinion.

c) The questions in Part 1 are personal and you should not interact with your partner. In Part 4 the questions are more general and you should discuss them with your partner.

d) The examiner may ask you a question directly, or ask a question to both of you. In either situation, you can give your own opinion by speaking alone, then invite your partner to say something if you want to.

e) You should say as much as you want to. You may have a lot of ideas, or only a few, but there is no right amount of time to speak in Part 4. However, it's a good idea to bring your partner into the discussion.

2a Answering the question. Work in pairs. Complete the dialogues about city centres with phrases from the box.

> always thought   I feel strongly about   never really thought about it
> seems to me   sure that is

a) Is it a good idea to ban traffic from city centres?
It .... that it would solve quite a few problems.

b) Should there be more parking in city centres?
I've .... as I don't have a car, …

c) What do you think about out of town shopping malls?
Well, ... supporting independent shops, …

d) Do you think shopping has become a social activity?
I'm .... the case.

e) Do you think cities are good places to live in?
I've .... that.

2b **Now match the example or reason to the answers in exercise 2a.**

1   … because we all enjoy meeting friends for shopping – we can have fun.

2   I think there are so many different things to do in cities!

3   … because we would use public transport more and we could have pedestrian areas in the city centre.

4   … because they are disadvantaged by the big chain stores.

5   … but I suppose it would help congestion and encourage people to visit the city.

> **Boost your grade!**
>
> You should always give your opinion and try to support it with an example.

3   **Engaging in discussion. Work in pairs. Put the phrases into the correct column.**

Interrupting politely	Asking for clarification	Getting your partner to say more
Sorry to interrupt, but …		

Could you explain what you mean?

So why do you think that?

Sorry, could you say that again?

That's interesting – can you give me an example?

That's a good point, but could I add something?

Can I say something?

Can you say a bit more about that?

What did you mean when you said …?

4a 🎧 ²/₃ **Listen to two students discussing the first two questions about holidays. Tick the phrases they use from exercise 3.**

a)   Do you think it's important to have a holiday every year? Why / Why not?

b)   Some people prefer to have one long holiday and others prefer to have several short holidays during the year. What's your opinion?

c)   Is it more fun to go on holiday with friends, or with family? Why?

d)   Some people say it's more fun to go on holiday in another country. What do you think?

e)   Is it better to relax on holiday, or do lots of different activities? Why?

f)   What's the best time of year to have a holiday? Why?

4b   **Work in pairs. Discuss the remaining questions. Remember to give your own opinion.**

> **Boost your grade!**
>
> Make sure you talk to your partner and don't just respond to the examiner's questions.
>
> Expand your answers whenever possible and try to include your partner in the discussion.

READING AND USE OF ENGLISH

Part 1

For questions **1–8**, read the text below and decide which answer (**A**, **B**, **C** or **D**) best fits each gap. There is an example at the beginning **(0)**.

Mark your answers **on the separate answer sheet**.

0   **A** gets   **B** does   **C** makes   **D** goes

0	A	B	C	D
	☐	☐	▬	☐

Is there or isn't there?

Every year it seems this question **(0)** .... the news again. Is there, or isn't there life on Mars? Some experts believe there used to be but now there isn't; others believe there still might be. And they send more tiny robots to the red planet in order to prove their **(1)** .... one way or another. It boils down to whether there was or **(2)** .... is water there. Photographs taken from craft orbiting the planet have shown that Mars has not always been dry and **(3)** .... Today the **(4)** .... of Mars would not support life, but there could be water **(5)** .... underground. First, **(6)** ...., scientists need to land a craft on Mars to prepare the way for future robots to investigate and that is proving quite a **(7)** .... Whatever is found there in the future is more likely to be tiny microorganisms **(8)** .... than anything more advanced. So, no little green men – at least, not on this particular planet!

1	**A** possibilities	**B** tests	**C** guesses	**D** theories
2	**A** even	**B** still	**C** yet	**D** already
3	**A** dusty	**B** dirty	**C** smooth	**D** littered
4	**A** top	**B** lining	**C** surface	**D** level
5	**A** long	**B** profound	**C** distant	**D** deep
6	**A** however	**B** but	**C** deep	**D** whereas
7	**A** worry	**B** challenge	**C** fight	**D** contest
8	**A** instead	**B** alternative	**C** better	**D** rather

Part 2

For questions **9–16**, read the text below and think of the word which best fits each gap. Use only one word in each gap. There is an example at the beginning **(0)**.

Write your answers **IN CAPITAL LETTERS on the separate answer sheet**.

Example:

0	T	H	E												

Anyone for shopping?

It is probably no surprise that shopping is **(0)** .... third most popular leisure activity today. Whether it's shopping online

(9) .... spending hours in shopping malls, we enjoy the

shopping experience. However, physical stores **(10)** ....

had to make big changes to entice us away from shopping websites

(11) .... the convenience of a one-click purchase is so

tempting and **(12)** .... we compare shopping malls today

with those a decade ago, the difference is really significant. Statistics

show **(13)** .... a third of people visiting shopping

malls today are not there to shop, but to eat. An enormous range of

restaurants and cafés offer exciting dining experiences and a chance

for socialising and catching **(14)** .... with friends.

And malls are bringing other aspects **(15)** .... the

leisure industry into these areas; for example in the summer some

buy in tons of sand to create whole beach areas in front of the mall.

What next? Now, there's **(16)** .... question.

Don't look for difficulty. Sometimes the words in the gaps are straight-forward. If it makes sense, it's probably correct.

Both of these gaps contain the same type of word. What kind of word do you think it is?

Part 3

For questions **17–24**, read the text below. Use the word given in capitals at the end of some of the lines to form a word that fits in the gap in the same line. There is an example at the beginning **(0)**.

Write your answers **IN CAPITAL LETTERS on the separate answer sheet**.

Example: | 0 | R | E | S | P | O | N | S | I | B | L | I | T | Y | | | | |

Dogs for therapy

Pets are good for us, we've known that for a long time. Having a pet

encourages young children to take on **(0)** .... and also   **RESPONSIBLE**

provide us with company and **(17)** .... Dogs have   **AFFECT**

also been used for years as guide dogs for people with **(18)** ....   **SEE**

problems and more **(19)** .... as service dogs for people with   **RECENT**

other **(20)** .... such as hearing loss. These dogs are specially   **ABILITY**

trained to perform tasks to make others' lives easier. However, a dog does

not always need special **(21)** .... in order to help others.   **TRAIN**

Stroking a dog can relieve stress and **(22)** ...., and dogs that   **TENSE**

are calm around people can be registered as 'dogs for therapy' and taken

into hospitals to help the patients. Doctors believe that a therapy dog

visit relaxes patients and can lead to a **(23)** .... recovery!   **SPEED**

Watching fish swim **(24)** .... around a tank is also   **LAZY**

relaxing but so far fish haven't been added to the 'therapy' hospital

visit list, yet!

Part 4

For questions **25–30**, complete the second sentence so that it has a similar meaning to the first sentence, using the word given. **Do not change the word given.** You must use between **two** and **five** words including the word given. Here is an example **(0)**.

Example:

0   It's fine for students to eat in the classrooms at lunchtime.

   ALLOWED

   Students ....*are allowed to*........... eat in the classrooms at lunchtime.

---

25   It's a good idea to leave soon before the traffic gets bad.

   BETTER

   You .... leave soon before the traffic gets bad.

26   A man who was walking his dog found the bag.

   BY

   The bag .... a man who was walking his dog.

27   'Sit down Angela and get on with your work,' the teacher said.

   TO

   The teacher .... and get on with her work.

28   If my dad can't drive us to the concert we'll take the bus.

   UNLESS

   We'll take the bus to the concert .... us.

29   I shall need some more information before I can write a report.

   ENOUGH

   I haven't .... write the report.

30   This is my first visit to London.

   NEVER

   I .... London before.

Part 5

You are going to read part of a story in which a woman, Callie, arrives at a house in the country. For questions **31–36** choose the answer (**A**, **B**, **C** or **D**) which you think fits best according to the text.

Mark your answers **on the separate answer sheet**.

Miss Patten at home

When I pressed the tiny plastic button on the door frame I couldn't hear an answering chime inside the house so I pressed again. Once more I was greeted with silence from inside and I stood for a moment, wondering what to do next. I'd come a long way for this interview, changing trains twice and splashing out on a taxi from the station to this small house, hidden away in the middle of nowhere. I'd let the taxi go and my heels were beginning to hurt and I wished I'd worn something more sensible to come out to the country, but it was a London habit.

As there was still no sign of life inside the house I walked, hesitantly, round to the side and found a low wooden gate beyond which was what I assumed was a garden. It could just as well have been an enclosed stretch of woodland as it was as wild a piece of land as I've ever seen, with no neighbouring houses in sight; low trees and tall grasses competed with each other and the occasional bright red poppy to reach the sun. From somewhere came a voice. 'Come in, come in, I'm in the garden.'

I pushed open the gate, with a little difficulty as it had to swing over high grass, and found a trodden path leading round the back of the house. Miss Patten was sitting at a wooden table in the shade of an oak, with handwritten papers scattered over the table top next to a laptop computer. The lady, who I knew to be well over sixty, lived up to her reputation of eccentricity. She was wearing purple and red and looked every inch the picture of the successful children's writer that she was, with intelligent eyes behind big round spectacles and greying hair pulled back into a bun at the back of her head.

She smiled up at me and waved a heavily-ringed hand towards a garden chair beside her. 'It's Callie, isn't it? Sit down please, you make me feel inferior standing there in your city elegance!' she said and I immediately felt as if I'd done something wrong and was being told off by my mother. I sat carefully on the chair and took out my notebook before placing my briefcase at my feet. 'Help yourself to elderflower lemonade. I think you could do with a drink!'

'Thank you so much for agreeing to talk to me Miss Patten, I ...' But then the ringed hand covered mine and squeezed. She smiled. 'No one calls me Miss Patten darling – it's Kitty. And try to breathe, I'm not going to bite, you know.' I swallowed and tried again, but my voice was dry. 'Thank you Kitty ...' I gulped down some of the elderflower lemonade which was actually very refreshing. 'As you know, we're doing a feature on the most influential writers of the generation and I'm here to ask you some questions about your lifestyle and working habits.'

Kitty wasn't listening. She lifted her chin and waved her hand to silence me. 'Oh – that's amazing, don't you think?' she asked. 'Every evening, just as the sun's going down – one of the advantages of living here. They nest in the beech tree over there. And they wake me every morning too. Just
line 34 lovely. Now, you don't get **that** in the city, do you?' I sighed and put down my notebook. This was going to be just as hard as I'd thought.

31 How does the writer feel when there is no response to ringing the bell?

    A   regretful that she made the journey

    B   unsure what action to take

    C   disappointed that she has been let down

    D   unhappy that she changed her footwear

32 Where does she think the gate leads?

    A   to the garden of the cottage

    B   to the edge of a wood

    C   to a field of flowers

    D   to other houses

33 The writer thinks that the woman's appearance

    A   is very fashionable.

    B   reflects her age.

    C   is contrary to her expectations.

    D   is typical of her profession.

34 The way Miss Patten treats Callie makes her feel

    A   unimportant.

    B   offended.

    C   guilty.

    D   confused.

35 In the fifth paragraph Callie

    A   reminds Miss Patten why she is there.

    B   reassures Miss Patten that she is professional.

    C   compliments Miss Patten on her latest work.

    D   ignores Miss Patten's discomfort.

36 In line 34, 'that' refers to

    A   the sight of the sunset.

    B   the beauty of living in the countryside.

    C   the sound of birds.

    D   the place Callie lives.

Part 6

You are going to read an article about a young man, Noah. Six sentences have been removed from the article. Choose from the sentences **A–G** the one which fits each gap (**37–42**). There is one extra sentence you do not need to use.

Mark your answers **on the separate answer sheet**.

Noah

I remember the sound of my coach's voice as we neared the end of the race: 'Finish line coming up in 100 yards. Give it all you've got!' I heard my parents ringing a bell and cheering for me, as sweat and sunscreen poured down my back that hot, muggy June day.

As I completed my first 10K (a hilly 6.2-mile road race I'd trained hard for), my parents ran over and hugged me, and I was completely overcome with emotion. *Ho-ly COW*, I thought to myself. *I did it.* It would've been thrilling for anyone — but it was that much more exciting for me because I'm blind.

My parents have always told me that I could do anything, so when I asked if I could start running cross-country in kindergarten, they immediately said yes. **37** For the 10K, a running coach guided me with a tether, a ropelike string that attached my wrist to his. It was so liberating to finally be able to move my arms freely and work on my technique!

Since I was born blind, I've always had a different perspective on the world than other people, and I've always been determined to not let my blindness hold me back. **38** I love skiing and can handle double black diamond trails independently, with a guide calling directions into a radio-like device that I strap to my head.

I also race motorized boats, steering as my dad yells out instructions: 'Left! Right! Straight!'. I ride horses and tandem bikes, and have done gruelling 12-hour mountain hikes. Music is a big part of my life too: I sing and play guitar, drums, and piano — though it took my mom six years to find teachers who were willing to take on the challenge of working with me. Six years! That's one of the biggest problems with being blind. People think you'll be hard work. **39** Sometimes friends do too. For example, I've had a great time at sleepovers at my house, but no friend has ever invited me to sleep at his house even though it wouldn't be a problem if they did. **40** It takes a good friend to remember to stop and walk out with me.

People also put me in an awkward position sometimes by approaching me and asking 'Guess who?' I don't think they are trying to be unkind, but I wish that they would introduce themselves and say, 'Hi, Noah, it's me, so-and-so.' **41**

After completing that first 10K, I ran another one in Canada, and I'm preparing for a major hike on a portion of the Appalachian Trail. I also recently started a radio show on the local college station and began hosting an online gathering for teens who are blind or visually impaired. **42** I enjoy these activities and don't think of myself as any different from other kids who have a variety of interests.

And while I feel proud when I defy others' expectations, I don't do things just to prove myself to others. I'm trying to live life to the fullest. The only limit that you have is in your mind. If you say, 'I can't do this, I can't do that,' well, no you can't. But if you say 'I can try,' then you've opened up a door, and you can keep opening doors rather than shutting them.

A It isn't just adults who make those assumptions, though.

B That's a little step that would go so far towards including a blind person in the conversation.

C I don't get annoyed when people ask me things. I want to answer them! It helps enlighten people and get rid of stereotypes.

D Running isn't my only hobby.

E And then there are the moments like the start of recess at school, when everyone goes sprinting out the door.

F We have fun discussing everything from school to technology.

G My dad held my hand as we ran, warning me as we approached curbs or turns and as the terrain changed from gravel to tar to hills.

Boost your grade!

1 Work in pairs. Read the text and sentences A–G and underline any words that refer to people and free-time activities.

2 Many of the words that you have underlined are clues to matching the sentences in this task. Look at the list of words/phrases from sentences A–G. These are all clues. Complete the list with the word or phrase in the text which links to these clues. Which sentence (A-G) does each item come from?

a) not just adults	(paragraph 5)	*A*	*friends too*
b) Running is not my only hobby	(paragraph 4)		
c) Everyone goes sprinting out of the door	(paragraph 5)		
d) We	(paragraph 7)		
e) my dad	(paragraph 1)		
f) terrain changed from gravel to tar to hills	(paragraph 1)		

Part 7

You are going read about four people's early memories of school. For questions **43–52** choose from the sections (**A–D**). The sections may be chosen more than once.

Mark your answers **on the separate answer sheet**.

Which writer

differed from most children in her attitude to school?

| 43 | |

blames her early school for a **current** attitude?

| 44 | |

> Only one text talks about the writer's 'current' lifestyle – which one?

later regretted her actions at school?

| 45 | |

now appreciates the problems she caused?

| 46 | |

recognises the **positive** influence early school had on her life?

| 47 | |

> Only one text describes positive memories of school – which one?

diverted attention from the lesson focus?

| 48 | |

dealt with a situation in an uncharacteristic manner?

| 49 | |

was **regularly** disciplined?

| 50 | |

> Two texts talk about discipline, but only one talks about 'regular' disciplining – which one?

corrects a **misconception** related to her first school?

| 51 | |

was befriended by a teacher?

| 52 | |

> Does 'misconception' mean an idea that turned out to be true or untrue? (The clue is in the prefix 'mis–'.)

A I can only have been about five years old so what I'm remembering is from my primary school which I now know was just a stone's throw from our old house. In fact it's only about a five-minute walk, but to short legs back then it seemed a long way, particularly when it was a walk you didn't want to make. I resented going to school and the idea that I had to be dressed in the same skirt and jumper as everyone else with the same black shoes, which weren't even allowed to be shiny. I hated that there was a bell that ruled every aspect of the school day. Those early experiences of conforming have coloured my life ever since and I chose a profession where I could be my own boss and not need to follow rules and times or wear anything remotely similar to anyone else.

B What I remember about my first school was being very naughty and causing my parents a lot of worry. They got called into the school to speak to my teachers more than once and for that I was punished by not being allowed to watch my favourite TV shows. My naughtiness, however, wasn't serious – I just found concentrating on lessons that weren't particularly interesting very difficult. So I would pass notes, chat to my friends, tell jokes in class and so on. I guess I was a distraction for the other students and the teachers weren't happy about that. I think I spent more time standing in the corridor outside the head teacher's room than actually in class. I'm a teacher myself now and I can see that I must have been a real pain.

C Those first years in education were brilliant and that is definitely down to the teacher we had. A good teacher can change a kid's life I think, particularly their attitude to studying and that has an effect on the next ten or twelve years of school. I just have this wonderful memory of wanting to go to school in the morning and of a feeling of dread when the holidays were approaching. My parents thought I was a bit mad, well at least a rather unusual child. But every morning I looked forward to that warm smile from our teacher, Miss Dunne, and trying to do my best to please her. She was the one who, on the very first day at school, when I was scared and worrying that no one was going to want to play with me, held my hand all through playtime and gave me the confidence to want to return the following day.

D I'm not a violent person. However, one of my earliest school memories is of biting another child. He was a bully, although at that time I didn't have the word in my vocabulary. He liked to push other kids around and one day he kicked my friend Helen and made her cry. I did something instinctive. I reached forward and bit him on the hand as hard as I could. He was so surprised he could hardly speak. I remember his eyes getting very big and then he started crying. For a moment I felt very good, that is until my dad was called to the school to take me home because of fighting. I remember feeling how unfair it was but after a long lecture about how to react to violence I felt a bit ashamed but it was still hard to apologise the following day.

WRITING

Part 1

You **must** answer this question. Write your answer in **140–190** words in an appropriate style on the separate answer sheet.

---

1 In your English class you have been talking about how much television young people watch, and whether watching television is a good thing. Now, your English teacher has asked you to write an essay.

Write your essay using **all** the notes and giving reasons for your point of view.

> Do young people watch too much television in their leisure time, and is watching television a good thing?
>
> **Notes**
>
> Write about:
>
> 1. needing to relax
> 2. using technology
> 3. .... (your own idea)

 THINK IT THROUGH

Remember to include an introduction to tell the reader what you are going to write about and a conclusion which summarises your argument.

Part 2

Write an answer to one of the questions **2–4** in this part. Write your answer in **140–190** words in an appropriate style on the separate answer sheet. Put the question number in the box at the top of the answer sheet.

2   You see this announcement in an English-language technology magazine.

> **Articles wanted**
>
> ### A memorable and important happy moment from your childhood
>
> What moment do you remember from your childhood? Why was it important?
>
> Write us an article answering these questions.
>
> We will print the most interesting articles in our magazine.

Write your **article**.

3   You have received this email from your friend Carlos.

> **From:** Carlos
>
> **Subject:** Advice on music festival
>
> Hi! I'm coming to the annual music festival in your town. I know you go every year, so can you give me some advice? I'd like to see as many bands as possible, but don't know who's playing.
>
> I haven't got a ticket yet so where can I buy one? Also, I need somewhere to stay. Can you recommend a cheap place?
>
> I'm looking forward to it, and hope to see you there.
>
> Carlos

Write your **email**.

4   You see this announcement on a website selling books.

> **Book reviews wanted**
>
> We want reviews of books with interesting characters and an exciting story!
>
> Write a review of a book you have read, telling us about the characters and saying what was exciting about the story. Would you recommend this book to other people?
>
> The best reviews will appear on our website.

Write your **review**.

 Your review should be engaging and must include your own opinion.

LISTENING

Part 1

You will hear people talking in eight different situations. For questions **1–8**, choose the best answer (**A**, **B**, or **C**).

1   You hear two students talking about music classes they attend at school.
What do they agree about?

   A   how entertaining it is to compose music

   B   how interesting it is to listen to new music

   C   how challenging it is to play an instrument

> There are two things to listen for here: the students' feelings and whether they are discussing composing, listening or playing.

2   You hear a man telling his friend about snowboarding.
He says that what he **enjoys** most about it is

   A   trying to beat his best times.

   B   entering competitions.

   C   learning new tricks.

> If the man is enjoying snowboarding, what words might he might he use to describe his feelings? Listen for these or similar words in the dialogue.

3   You hear a woman talking about making jewellery as a hobby.
She says that she started doing it because she

   A   didn't like what was already available.

   B   wanted a new challenge.

   C   likes being creative.

4   You hear a man talking about writing stories.
What advice does he offer?

   A   read a lot of other stories

   B   consider the ending carefully

   C   make sure characters are believable

> The man gives lots of advice, but only one piece of advice matches one of the options.

5   You hear two friends talking about a music magazine they both read.
What does the girl say about it?

   A   She wishes it included more interviews.

   B   She isn't keen on the free gifts.

   C   She likes its design.

The girl mentions all of these things. Check carefully - does she say she likes or dislikes each one?

6   You hear a young man talking about his part-time job.
How does he feel about it?

   A   nervous about working with older people

   B   pleased with the working conditions

   C   surprised by how quickly he is learning to do it

What does 'working conditions' mean? Can you think of any examples?

7   You hear a teacher talking to his class.
What is the purpose of his talk?

   A   to remind the students to do something

   B   to warn the students against doing something

   C   to praise the students for something they've done

8   You hear two friends talking about a party they are going to.
What is she unsure about?

   A   what she ought to take

   B   how she will get there

   C   when it will finish

What phrases might the teacher use to remind, warn or praise students?

Part 2

 You will hear a young woman called Steffi talking about doing a walk in the mountains.

For questions **9–18**, complete the sentences with a word or short phrase.

Walking in the mountains

Steffi did a walk called the '**(9)** ....'.

The route Steffi did had **(10)** .... for people to hold.

The reason Steffi did the walk was to see the **(11)** .... she had heard about.

Steffi had taken her own **(12)** .... to wear on the walk.

Steffi liked seeing **(13)** .... on her way up the mountain.

When Steffi climbed a ladder, she felt **(14)** .... but the feeling soon passed.

Steffi says that the part of the walk they did after lunch appeared more **(15)** .... than it really was.

Steffi compares the rocks she saw on the valley floor with **(16)** ....

When she reached the bottom of the mountain after an activity called abseiling, Steffi felt

(17) ....

The walk Steffi would really like to do includes seeing **(18)** .... as part of the trip.

 THINK IT THROUGH

Pay attention to your spelling. Even if you have heard the information correctly, you may lose marks for a word that is incorrectly spelt.

Part 3

You will hear five short extracts in which people are talking about their ambitions. For questions **19–23**, choose from the list (**A–H**) what each speaker says about why they want to achieve their ambition. Use the letters only once. There are three extra letters which you do not need to use.

A   I want to learn a new skill.

B   I want to entertain other people.

C   I want to push myself to the limit.

Speaker 1	19
Speaker 2	20
Speaker 3	21
Speaker 4	22
Speaker 5	23

D   I want to have as much fun as I can.

E   I want to prove myself to someone.

F   I want to achieve fame and fortune.

G   I want to understand more about life.

H   I want to make a difference to the world.

Boost your grade!

1   **The following sentences are used in the listening task. Can you complete them with the words from the recording?**

a) 'I'm going to find out what I'm .... of.'

b) 'I have a brilliant time .... with my mates.'

c) 'I'm not sure anyone takes me .... , I'm going to show them!'

d) 'I just want to contribute something to ....'

e) 'Travel .... the mind.'

2   **Now write a paraphrase for each sentence. Use sentences A–H to help you.**

Part 4

You will hear an interview with a woman called Carly Smith, who is talking about taking part in a TV talent competition.

For questions **24–30**, choose the best answer (**A**, **B**, or **C**).

---

24 Carly applied for the TV talent show because

A   she wanted to show people what she could do.

B   she had enjoyed watching a previous series of it.

C   she thought it would be an exciting thing to take part in.

25 How did Carly feel after her audition?

A   pleased she hadn't made any mistakes in her performance

B   concerned about whether the judges liked her performance

C   keen to improve certain aspects of her performance

26 How did Carly spend her time before the live TV shows started?

A   attempting to make her performance unique

B   carrying out some visualisation techniques

C   keeping herself as relaxed as possible

27 What did Carly feel most nervous about before her first live show?

A   the closeness of the TV cameras

B   the reactions of the studio audience

C   the physical conditions of the studio

28 As Carly waited for the judge's decision, she felt

A   hopeful of persuading them to accept her for the next round.

B   embarrassed about having given a poor performance.

C   certain she would be voted out of the competition.

29 When Carly was put through to the second live show, she realised that

A   she still had a lot of hard work to do.

B   she wasn't keen to continue in the competition.

C   she felt more pleased than she'd expected.

30 How did Carly feel after her final performance on the show?

A   relieved that the process was over

B   confident that her skills had improved

C   sad to say goodbye to fellow participants

How to ... deal with distractors

1 **Choose one synonym for each of the words 1–7.**

1 exciting
a) thrilling   b) appealing   c) loving

2 concerned
a) enjoyed   b) hopeful   c) worried

3 unique
a) unexpected   b) unusual   c) ultimate

4 put (me) off
a) made me nervous   b) concerned me   c) disturbed me

5 persuade
a) accept   b) influence   c) compare

6 quit
a) stop   b) prepare   c) continue

7 regret
a) challenge   b) be sorry   c) be relieved

> **Boost your grade!**
>
> In Part 4 you listen to a monologue or dialogue. You may be asked about:
> - the speaker's name, job or hobby
> - the setting (e.g. a TV interview)
> - the speaker's attitude, opinion or feelings
> - specific information

2 **Look at the transcript on page 127 and check your answers.**

3 **Look at question 24 on page 90 again. Read the first part of the transcript for this question below and read the notes that the student has made. Which is the correct option? Which of the underlined phrases are distractors and why are they wrong?**

Talking about what she is capable of? Option A?

I saw an advert about applying and thought, why not give it a go? I've done acrobatics since I was a kid – which is like gymnastics, except it doesn't rely on equipment and is more about performance. I love it! The TV competition took place over three weeks and each week judges voted for participants and someone got knocked out. I hadn't paid a lot of attention to that before so I'm not sure why it suddenly appealed to me but it seemed like a thrilling thing to get involved in.

Does 'thrilling' mean 'exciting'? Option C?

Something which happened previously? Option B?

4 **Look at question 29 again. Read part of the transcript for this question below and underline the distractors and what Carly says which gives you the answer.**

I'd put so much energy into that first performance and then I suddenly thought I'm going to have to do something different now. I hadn't thought that far ahead. So, although on the one hand, I was delighted to have got through, another part of me briefly wondered how I was going to carry on. I never seriously considered quitting, but as there was only a week to prepare this time, I knew I'd better get my ideas together quickly.

? THINK IT THROUGH

Distractors are words which are similar to the words used in the recording but are included to lead you away from the correct option. Look carefully at the words that come with these distractors, e.g. *mainly*, *all*, *everybody*, or negatives such as ***didn't*** like, ***un****happy*, to help you decide on the correct answer.

SPEAKING

Part 1 (2 minutes)

Select one or more questions from any of the following categories, as appropriate.

Everyday life

- Which day of the week do you prefer? (Why?)
- Do you like to have a routine, or do you prefer to be spontaneous? (Why?)
- Do you have a busy life? (Why / Why not?)
- What is your favourite time of day? (Why?)

Friends and family

- Do you usually go out with friends in the evenings or at weekends? (Why?)
- Tell us something about your family.
- Do you share the same interests as all your friends?
- Do you often chat to your friends on social media? (Why / Why not?)

Technology

- What is your favourite piece of technology? (Why?)
- What do you use your mobile phone for most? (Why?)
- Is it important for you to have the latest mobile phone? (Why / Why not?)
- Would you be able to live without technology? (Why / Why not?)

Part 2 (4 minutes)

In this part of the test you are going to have two photographs. You have to talk about your photographs on your own for about a minute, and also answer a question about your partner's photographs.

Candidate A: Here are your photographs. They show **people studying in different places**.

Compare the photographs, and say **why you think the people have decided to study in these places**.

Why have the people decided to study in these places?

(Candidate B), **which of these places would you prefer to study in? (Why?)**

Candidate B: Here are your photographs. They show **people spending a day out near the sea**.

Compare the photographs and say **what you think the people are enjoying about spending a day out near the sea**.

> **What are the people enjoying about spending a day out near the sea?**

(Candidate A), **do you enjoy being by the sea? Why / Why not?**

You have 15 seconds to look at the task. Think about how the prompts link to the question.

Part 3 (4 minutes)

Now, you have to talk about something together for about two minutes.

Here are some ways young people often get advice about their future career, and a question for you to discuss.

Now talk to each other about **whether these are good ways for young people to get advice about their future career**.

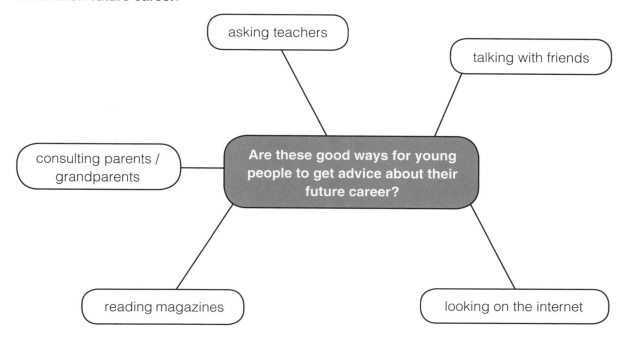

asking teachers

talking with friends

consulting parents / grandparents

Are these good ways for young people to get advice about their future career?

reading magazines

looking on the internet

Now you have about a minute to decide **which is the most effective way for young people to get the best advice about their future career**.

Part 4 (4 minutes)

Answer these questions.

- Is it important for young people to plan their future careers carefully? (Why / Why not?)

- Do you think it's generally easy for young people to get good advice nowadays? (Why / Why not?)

- Do you think it's usually better to listen to advice from other people, or make your own decisions? (Why?)

- Which do you think is most important for a career, qualifications or experience? (Why?)

- Some people say there are too many pressures on young people these days. Do you agree? (Why / Why not?)

- What's the best piece of advice you've ever been given? (Why?)

READING AND USE OF ENGLISH

Part 1

For questions **1–8**, read the text below and decide which answer (**A**, **B**, **C** or **D**) best fits each gap. There is an example at the beginning **(0)**.

Mark your answers **on the separate answer sheet**.

0   **A** heard   **B** listened   **C** spoken   **D** learned

0	A	B	C	D
	■	▭	▭	▭

Soul Kitchen

Most people have **(0)** .... of Jon Bon Jovi, the rock singer. What is perhaps less well known is the fact that he and his wife have **(1)** .... a lot of time and money to helping homeless people and those on very **(2)** .... incomes. There are two restaurants so **(3)** .... called *Soul Kitchen* which are classed as 'Pay it forward' community restaurants. This **(4)** .... they serve nutritious meals to both paying customers and those who cannot **(5)** .... to pay. Paying customers buy meals for themselves and pay for a future meal for those who don't have enough money. There are also opportunities for those in **(6)** .... to volunteer at the restaurant and **(7)** .... get training in the food industry. There are similar schemes in other places too – *The Social Bite in Scotland* is one. George Clooney **(8)** .... focused media attention on one of the Scottish branches when he visited several years ago.

1	**A** gifted	**B** donated	**C** dedicated	**D** made
2	**A** poor	**B** short	**C** light	**D** low
3	**A** far	**B** long	**C** now	**D** good
4	**A** mentions	**B** means	**C** says	**D** refers
5	**A** incline	**B** make	**C** afford	**D** have
6	**A** desire	**B** want	**C** necessity	**D** need
7	**A** even	**B** yet	**C** still	**D** ever
8	**A** lately	**B** recently	**C** presently	**D** immediately

THINK IT THROUGH

Always read the text all the way through first, ignoring the gaps, to get the general idea of what it is about.

Part 2

For questions **9–16**, read the text below and think of the word which best fits each gap. Use only one word in each gap. There is an example at the beginning **(0)**.

Write your answers **IN CAPITAL LETTERS on the separate answer sheet**.

Example: | 0 | *I* | *N* | | | | | | | | | | | | | | |

Low-tech solution

Drones have become very popular **(0)** .... recent years. They are used officially **(9)** .... the military and there are even plans for delivery companies to use **(10)** .... to deliver packages. However, one of the main reasons why there are more and more drones in our skies **(11)** .... because flying them has become a major hobby for a lot of people. Yet, there is a problem with this exciting hobby. Sometimes the drones present a real danger by **(12)** .... flown too close to airports. **(13)** .... **issue** is that they may fly over restricted, sensitive areas or even during state visits where security is vital. The Dutch police have **(14)** .... up with a clever way of taking out drones that present potential problems – using eagles to catch the drones and destroy them. These large birds are trained to identify the drones **(15)** .... prey. Until a cleverer high-tech solution can be **(16)** .... this natural answer could be very effective.

What will the word in gap 10 refer back to? Should it be singular or plural?

If you take 'why there are more and more drones in our skies' (relative clause) out of this sentence, you'll see there is a key word missing from the sentence. What is it?

issue = problem
We have read about one problem. What is it? The word in this gap introduces a further issue.

THINK IT THROUGH

Three of these gaps require you to have a good knowledge of how passive tenses work. Which three?

Part 3

For questions **17–24**, read the text below. Use the word given in capitals at the end of some of the lines to form a word that fits in the gap in the same line. There is an example at the beginning **(0)**.

Write your answers **IN CAPITAL LETTERS on the separate answer sheet**.

Example: | 0 | S | T | U | D | E | N | T | S | | | | | | | | |

University or an apprenticeship?

For years, going to university has seemed the best option for **(0)** .... **STUDY**

who are leaving school. The **(17)** .... they receive after three or **QUALIFY**

more years of full-time study should help them find employment and the chance

to have a **(18)** .... and enjoyable career. Today's students **PROFIT**

tuition fees, **(19)** .... in the UK, are getting higher. Apprenticeships, **SPECIAL**

where you work for a company while studying for a degree, are becoming more

popular. The cost of studying is paid by the **(20)** .... and the **EMPLOY**

government. It's hard work and in **(21)** .... it means that the **ADD**

students don't get the benefit of the university experience, but many

apprentices say that the advantages of working and studying at the same time

outweigh the **(22)** .... The degrees they gain are as **ADVANTAGE**

(23) .... to future employers as those gained at a university and **ACCEPT**

the experience of working could **(24)** .... help when applying **ACTUAL**

for a job.

Part 4

For questions **25–30**, complete the second sentence so that it has a similar meaning to the first sentence, using the word given. **Do not change the word given.** You must use between **two** and **five** words including the word given. Here is an example **(0)**.

Example:

0 It's fine for students to eat in the classrooms at lunchtime.

ALLOWED

Students ....*are allowed to*................ eat in the classrooms at lunchtime.

---

25 I didn't go to the Louvre when I was on holiday in Paris and now I regret it.

WISH

I .... to the Louvre when I was on holiday in Paris.

26 The police had closed the road after the accident.

BY

The road .... the police after the accident.

27 The museum staff didn't let anyone touch the exhibits.

WAS

No one .... touch the exhibits in the museum.

28 I started work on this project at 9 o'clock this morning and I still haven't finished.

WORKING

I .... on this project since 9 o'clock this morning.

29 I didn't do my assignment until the following day because I was too busy.

PUT

I .... my assignment until the following day because I was too busy.

30 Leo went to bed early because he didn't want to be tired the next morning.

THAT

Leo went to bed early .... be tired the next morning.

Part 5

You are going to read part of a story an editor's journey home. For questions **31–36** choose the answer (**A**, **B**, **C** or **D**) which you think fits best according to the text.

Mark your answers **on the separate answer sheet**.

The editor

The soon-to-be-dead editor moved importantly along the platform, squat and puffed up like a baby bird. He was reflecting on the satisfying number of authors he had patronised during the day. His nose twitched as he recalled a particularly witty remark he'd made to an inexperienced new writer that afternoon; he enjoyed putting people in their place. His view and vision of their work was by far more important than their own. He was, after all, the expert. And how delightful the gossip had been with his colleagues. Our editor liked to share his little triumphs. On form, his wit could be as sharp as a stand-up comedians. Many colleagues (he didn't have 'friends' as such) had commented in passing to each other (only 'in passing' as their interest in him didn't warrant full conversations) that he might do the publishing world a service and pursue an alternative career on the stage.

line 11 The tube arrived. It was heaving as usual, but a delicate manoeuvre, uncharacteristic for a person of his shape and size, gained him a seat. He smiled in a superior way at the large woman he had beaten to the prize, balanced his briefcase carefully on his knees and sat back to relive his successes of the day. His pale, fat cheeks creased in a self-satisfied smile as he replayed his one sided conversations.

'Well. Someone's had a good day then,' a voice remarked.

The editor looked up, unsure whether the voice was addressing him. He didn't want to be addressed. In his opinion, tube trains were not places for conversations, particularly with strangers. Strangers were unaware of how important he was, how good at his job and how bright his future was in the publishing world. He moved in different circles to most people on the tube. It was bad enough having to sit beside them, fight for seats with them and breathe the same air. The owner of the voice was a woman in black. She was tall, thin and appeared to be standing without the assistance of the handles or poles. The editor breathed in sharply. She might actually fall onto him when the tube screamed round a bend. His self-satisfied smile froze.

'Yes, you.' she said as if he had spoken. She was pale but everything else about her was dark. 'I think that was a smile on your face. Unusual to see even a tiny smile in the Friday rush hour.'

Our editor gave a brief nod and dropped his eyes. The classic, inoffensive retreat from unwanted interaction. With luck she would get the message that he was not the sort of person who conversed on tubes and move those dark eyes somewhere else – oh yes, and hold onto a handle. Please, he begged her silently, hold onto the rail.

'I've had a bad day. Can you tell?' a little pricking on the back of his neck told him that the strange lady was not getting the message at all. He shifted his weight from one side to another *line 33* and studied his briefcase. 'This isn't make up you know. It's anger. Some people go red when they're angry. Not me. I go white. I've had a very bad day.' Her voice seemed a lot closer. The editor risked a quick look and found her eyes almost on a level with his. She was actually bending over to look at him. And, she was still unsupported. His heart jumped and his eyes moved round to see how many people were watching at this strange event. Unsurprisingly everyone else squashed in the carriage had better things to do with their time. 'My anger sits inside me like a block of ice. Does anger get you like that?' she asked quietly.

31   Why is the editor feeling good in the first paragraph?

   A   he's impressed his boss

   B   he's made some good decisions

   C   he's decided on a good career move

   D   he's got what he wanted

32   In line 11, 'heaving' implies that the underground train

   A   was moving.

   B   was crowded.

   C   was delayed.

   D   was noisy.

33   On the train the editor was concerned that a passenger

   A   might lose her balance.

   B   might recognise him.

   C   might not respect him.

   D   might sit next to him.

34   The editor wanted the woman to realise

   A   that he did not like her.

   B   that he didn't usually travel by tube.

   C   that he wanted to be alone.

   D   that he didn't intend to offend her.

35   'This' in line 33 refers to

   A   the woman's emotion.

   B   the woman's face.

   C   the woman's clothes.

   D   the woman's reaction.

36   Why is he surprised in the final paragraph?

   A   the woman's actions haven't been noticed

   B   the woman is falling

   C   the woman's very close to him

   D   the woman is angry

Sometimes you get a question which focuses on the meaning of one word in the text. If you don't know the word, use the context around the word to help you make a sensible guess. In this example, the rest of the sentence in the text goes on to describe what the man has to do because the train is 'heaving'. Does reading this help you to decide what the word means?

Part 6

You are going to read an article about a young woman, from an unusual cultural background. Six sentences have been removed from the article. Choose from the sentences **A–G** the one which fits each gap (**37–42**). There is one extra sentence you do not need to use.

Mark your answers **on the separate answer sheet**.

Should teens do extreme sports?

The summer before my senior year of high school, during a four-week science program at the University of California, Davis, I was eating in a cafeteria with some other high school students and this one girl asks me: 'Do you live in a teepee?' **37** I said, 'Are you serious?' She said, 'Oh, wait, I'm sorry. Is that something I shouldn't ask?' I know she wasn't trying to be rude, so it didn't bother me. I just said, 'No, I have a house with electricity and running water. I'm not disconnected from the world!' But the truth is, I did grow up differently.

I'm a Native American and I'm from a reservation in Arizona. A reservation is a place that's reserved for Native American tribes by the federal government. Some reservations (like the 16 million-acre Navajo Nation in Arizona, New Mexico and Utah) are huge, while others are just over one acre in size. Mine is on the smaller side. People often have misconceptions about what living on a reservation means. **38** In reality, though, my life probably looks a lot like yours. There are paved roads and restaurants. Oh, and I'm obsessed with basketball! I was named MVP of my league senior year and now that I'm a freshman in college, I play intramural hoops.

Even though I consider myself a typical teen, there are definitely ways that my life has been different. **39** Our house is surrounded by a mountain, a river and a farm. We have 23 animals: ten chickens, four goats, four dogs, three cats, a guinea pig and a horse. It's not just for show! We collect eggs from the chickens, use manure from the animals to fertilize soil and pick fruits and vegetables from our garden. I've also learned how to hunt and fish.

My tribe is also known for its weaving and beadwork. I love making all sorts of fun accessories, like earrings, barrettes, and necklaces – it's my way of relaxing at the end of a long day. When I'm at school I wear my beadwork around campus. A lot of kids will ask, 'Where did you get those earrings?' **40** It makes me feel special.

Going to college has been a big change for me. There were only 25 people in my graduating class, and now I go to school with thousands. On my reservation, I was surrounded mostly by Natives, and at college, the Native population is only 0.07%. **41**

I'm studying to become a veterinarian – there aren't any on my reservation. If an animal gets sick, you have to drive an hour to get them help. My goal is to open a veterinary clinic that will help my reservation prosper. In fact, it's actually pretty rare for teens from where I grew up to go to college. We've been plagued by poverty – and that's pushed many toward drug and alcohol abuse. **42** It's important to me to eventually return to the reservation and invest in my tribe's future.

Which of the situations that the writer describes could be considered 'intimidating'?

A The reservation is an hour from town, so not only is there a strong community feel, but there's also a big connection to the land.

E About 56 million acres in the country are held for Native American tribes.

B It's **intimidating**, but also exciting.

F **But** I'm determined to become a positive role model for my reservation.

C **Some** think, for instance, that I wear a headdress and moccasins every day.

G It was such a silly question that, at first, I thought she was joking!

D When I say I made them, they can't believe it!

'Some' = some people

'But' introduces a contrast with what is said before.

THINK IT THROUGH

- Practise your grammar to help with your understanding of sentence structures.

- Read as much as you can to increase your vocabulary. Get into the habit of reading something in English every day. Choose something you know you will enjoy, such as a magazine or newspaper article, or a web page about something you are interested in or need to find out. Graded readers are a good option if you don't have the time or desire to read a full-length book. Check out our range of higher-level readers at www.scholasticeltreaders.com

Part 7

You are going read about four birthdays. For questions **43–52** choose from the sections (**A–D**). The sections may be chosen more than once.

Mark your answers **on the separate answer sheet**.

Which section mentions

someone impressed by another's generosity?   43 ☐

a surprise that wasn't well hidden?   44 ☐

a person who would have liked to have had some warning?   45 ☐

a **philosophical attitude** towards an unwanted gift?   46 ☐

> What does the writer say which shows a philosophical attitude?

a relaxed start to a birthday?   47 ☐

a **well-kept** secret?   48 ☐

> This adjective comes from 'keep a secret well'.

a serious misunderstanding?   49 ☐

uncharacteristic behaviour?   50 ☐

> Does 'uncharacteristic' mean 'typical' or 'not typical'?

careful and considerate preparations for a celebration?   51 ☐

unexpectedly good news?   52 ☐

> something unexpected = a surprise

A I'd known all day that something was on the cards. You know how it is when people are doing their best to pretend – and in this case it was to fake surprise that it was my birthday. 'Oh Jack – really? Why didn't you let anyone know?' said my boss when I handed round cupcakes at break time. But throughout the day I'd seen a large white envelope surreptitiously changing hands and peeking out from under a magazine. So when they presented me with the big card signed by everyone at work, including those on holiday (and I still don't know how they did that!), I had to act surprised. It was a lovely thought, as was the pair of theatre tickets they'd bought for me and Sally. It was just a shame we'd already seen it the previous week. Still, it's the thought that counts.

B Keeping a secret has never been easy for my sister. Her face usually gives her away – she can't look you directly in the eye and sometimes the tip of her nose goes pink. So, I was all the more impressed when I opened the front door to be greeted by 'Happy Birthday' being sung by a room full of friends and family. I couldn't speak, it was such a surprise – I just wish I hadn't come home straight from swimming club. My hair was dripping all over the place and I was wearing no make-up! But I got changed and we had an excellent party. Needless to say, Mum had cooked a lot of great food and my brother, who does DJing as a hobby, organised the music. The neighbours had been invited too, so there was no one to complain about the noise. My very best birthday ever.

C I shall never forget my thirtieth birthday. It had been a bad year as I'd lost a job that I loved because of the downsizing of the company. My fiancé, Laura, was amazing throughout that year and kept telling me life would get better and to stay optimistic and keep applying. I turned 30 on Saturday 18th March and I wasn't working that day, so I had a lie-in. Laura brought me the post in bed and I opened all the cards. We laughed at the funny ones and my Aunt Sarah had popped in a cheque too, which was really kind, seeing as she doesn't have much money herself. Then I came to a white, typed envelope. Inside was a letter informing me that I'd got the job I'd been interviewed for three weeks previously. I'd thought that I'd come off really badly in the interview so it was a wonderful surprise. Needless to say, Laura and I celebrated for a long time.

D It had been meticulously planned. Everything was organised down to the last detail. All my grandfather's favourite tracks from rock, through pop to hip-hop (which still astounds me!) were sequenced to reflect the different stages of his life (biker, artist, teacher) and would be played as the meal progressed. Every element of every dish held a certain memory too – after all it isn't every day you make it to 90 years old. The organisation had taken ages with countless visits and calls to the hotel as well as arranging accommodation for all the family coming over from the USA. And what happened. We drove up in a posh limousine with my grandfather for his birthday celebration to be told we'd got the date wrong. We'd accidentally booked the Saturday instead of the Friday!

WRITING

Part 1

You **must** answer this question. Write your answer in **140–190** words in an appropriate style on the separate answer sheet.

---

1   In your English class you have been talking about traffic problems in city centres. Now, your English teacher has asked you to write an essay.

Write your essay using **all** the notes and giving reasons for your point of view.

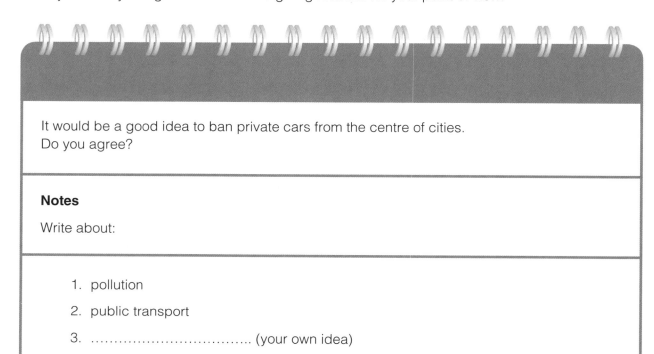

It would be a good idea to ban private cars from the centre of cities.
Do you agree?

Notes

Write about:

1. pollution
2. public transport
3. .... (your own idea)

THINK IT THROUGH

Remember to use formal language when you write an essay.

Part 2

Write an answer to one of the questions **2–4** in this part. Write your answer in **140–190** words in an appropriate style on the separate answer sheet. Put the question number in the box at the top of the answer sheet.

2   You see this announcement in an English-language technology magazine.

> **Reviews wanted!**
>
> We are looking for reviews of websites that our readers find particularly useful. Send us a review of your favourite website, describing the website and saying why you find it so useful.
>
> Tell us whether you would recommend it to other people.
>
> The best reviews will be published in the magazine.

Write your **review**.

3
> You recently took a short language course abroad, and you have been asked to write a report on the course for your own college website.
>
> You report should:
>
> • say what the classes were like
>
> • include information about what you learned
>
> • say whether you would recommend the course to other people

Write your **report**.

 THINK IT THROUGH

Report: Make sure you give reasons for your recommendations.

4   You see this announcement in an English-language sports magazine.

> **Articles wanted**
>
> We're running a series of articles on why sport is important in people's lives, called:
>
> *I couldn't live without sport!*
>
> We want articles from our readers about their experiences.
>
> Tell us what made you feel like that about sport, and the kind of sport you prefer.
>
> We will publish the best articles in the magazine.

Write your **article**.

LISTENING

Part 1

You will hear people talking in eight different situations. For questions **1–8**, choose the best answer (**A**, **B**, or **C**).

---

1   You hear two friends talking about learning to play a
       musical instrument.
       What do they **agree** about?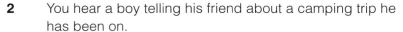

       A   how challenging it is

       B   how much fun it is

       C   how useful it is

 Listen for an opinion which both speakers give.

2   You hear a boy telling his friend about a camping trip he
       has been on.
       How did he feel before he went?

       A   concerned about it being boring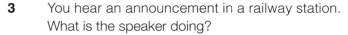

       B   nervous about the chosen location

       C   worried about using equipment

 As 'concerned', 'nervous' and 'worried' all have similar meanings, it is the second part of each option that you need to listen for.

3   You hear an announcement in a railway station.
       What is the speaker doing?

       A   introducing a new train service

       B   giving reasons for a cancellation

       C   advising passengers what to do

4   You hear a young man talking about learning to sing.
       How did he feel during his first lesson?

       A   surprised at how difficult reading music was

       B   excited about learning songs he recognised

       C   worried that he didn't have a nice voice

5   You hear two friends talking about a computer game one of them is playing.
     What is the boy's opinion of the game?

A   It requires a lot of concentration.

B   It doesn't last long enough.

C   It is fascinating to play.

6   You hear a woman talking about climbing a mountain.
     How did she feel when she reached the top?

A   thrilled to have achieved a lifelong ambition

B   delighted by her climbing progress

C   astonished by the view

 As 'thrilled', 'delighted' and 'astonished' are all used in similar ways, it is the second part of each option that you need to listen for.

7   You hear a woman leaving a phone message.
     Why is she calling?

A   to ask for a favour

B   to change an arrangement

C   to invite someone to an event

 The woman says 'Are you still going (to the party)'? The use of 'still' is significant. Which option do we now know is not correct?

8   You hear two friends reviewing a café they have been to.
     What does the man say about it?

A   The food was better than he expected.

B   The facilities were excellent.

C   The **atmosphere** was fun.

 What kind of thing might the man mention to describe the atmosphere?

Part 2

 You will hear a boy called Olly talking about setting up a band.

For questions **9–18**, complete the sentences with a word or short phrase.

Playing in a band

Olly says he wasn't **(9)** .... to learn the guitar at first.

Olly says that he didn't mind having to do his **(10)** ...., unlike other people he knew.

Olly didn't want to join the **(11)** .... in his home town as he didn't like the music.

Olly managed to find other musicians by putting an advert on a **(12)** ....

The band practise in the **(13)** .... of one the band member's homes.

The band decided to call themselves '**(14)** ....' .

Because they weren't good song writers, the band initially played what are known as

(15) .... songs.

The band's first concert took place at a **(16)** ....

Olly's favourite concert so far was at a **(17)** ....

The band are currently hoping to find a music **(18)** .... to help them.

 THINK IT THROUGH

Remember - only write words you hear on the recording.

PHOTOCOPIABLE

Part 3

 You will hear five short extracts in which people are talking about holidays they have been on. For questions **19–23**, choose from the list (**A–H**) what each speaker says they enjoyed most about the holiday. Use the letters only once. There are three extra letters which you do not need to use.

THINK IT THROUGH

Look carefully at the instructions above.

The speakers discuss each of these topics.

- their previous expectations about the holidays
- their hopes for the trip
- things they liked best about their holidays

Which of these topics will NOT help you answer questions 19–23?

A	studying history	
B	enjoying new food	Speaker 1 [ ] **19**
C	doing a new activity	Speaker 2 [ ] **20**
D	having time to relax	Speaker 3 [ ] **21**
E	meeting new people	Speaker 4 [ ] **22**
F	learning a new language	Speaker 5 [ ] **23**
G	visiting interesting places	
H	finding out about a new culture	

THINK IT THROUGH

After listening, look at the transcript on pages 129–130 and underline the phrases that the speakers use to express things they enjoyed and the best bits of their trip.

Part 4

 You will hear an interview with a young woman called Emma Holloway, who writes a blog.

For questions **24–30**, choose the best answer (**A**, **B**, or **C**).

24 Emma decided to start her blog because she thought that existing blogs

    A   were not very well written.

    B   were not particularly entertaining.

    C   were not aimed at a wide audience.

25 When Emma talks about finding readers for her blog, she expresses

    A   pride about how quickly it became popular.

    B   surprise at the way in which it got noticed.

    C   confidence in her writing abilities.

26 When Emma heard someone talking about her blog, she was

    A   too shocked to say anything.

    B   eager to find out more about who she was.

    C   worried about hearing something she didn't like.

27 Emma says that she gets her inspiration from

    A   books she reads.

    B   people she knows.

    C   things she overhears.

28 When Emma writes her blog, she tries to

    A   offer a new viewpoint on topics.

    B   identify with her target readers.

    C   answer questions about life.

29 What does Emma say about her future?

    A   She is undecided about what to do for work.

    B   She would like it to include writing in some way.

    C   She is concerned about running out of ideas for her blog.

30 What advice does Emma give to potential bloggers?

    A   Only write about familiar topics.

    B   Make an effort to avoid grammatical mistakes.

    C   Don't worry if people don't like what you do at first.

How to ... prepare for the Listening test

1   **Complete the descriptions about each part of the Listening test. Use the words in the boxes.**

> one (×2)   two   three (×3)   five   seven   eight (×2)
> ten   each (×2)   twice   exact   same

In **Part 1** you will hear **(1)** .... short unrelated extracts. There is **(2)** .... question per extract. Each question has **(3)** .... options. You will hear each extract **(4)** ....

In **Part 2** you will hear a monologue or **(5)** .... speakers talking for about **(6)** .... minutes. This part of the test is designed to check your ability to identify and understand specific information.

You need to complete **(7)** .... sentences with words from the listening. You must write the **(8)** .... words you hear. Unusual words or names may be spelt out by the speaker(s) and if so, you have to spell them correctly.

In **Part 3** there are **(9)** .... short monologues in which all the speakers talk about a similar topic. This part asks you to identify the general idea of what **(10)** .... speaker says, as well as information about their attitudes, relationships, opinions, etc.

There are more options than you need – **(11)** .... in total – but there is just **(12)** .... correct option per speaker.

In **Part 4** you have to answer **(13)** .... multiple choice questions about a monologue or short dialogue. There are **(14)** .... options to choose from and each recording lasts about three minutes.

The questions always follow the **(15)** .... order as the recording and **(16)** .... question relates to a specific section.

2   **Read the advice for each part of the Listening test. Think about your own experiences of taking practice Listening tests. Highlight one item in each list that is particularly important for you to remember.**

Part 1
- For each extract read the situation carefully and the question which follows it.
- As you listen, try to answer the question, and then check your ideas against the options.
- If you still don't know, decide which options are definitely NOT correct and then make a reasoned guess.

Part 2
- For each gap think about what kind of answer is likely, e.g. should you be listening for a name, place, number.
- Don't write down the first possible answer - make sure you listen to the whole section before you write.
- Be careful of distractors - there may be words, phrases or numbers which seem to fit the gap but are wrong.

Part 3
- Read the instructions and decide what the link is between each monologue.
- Underline the key words in each option.
- Think about the vocabulary related to the topic - what words might the speakers use?

Part 4
- Read the instruction and find out who you are going to be listening to and what the topic is.
- Listen for expressions with synonyms or antonyms to the words in the options. Beware of distractors!
- Listen to the whole section before you choose your answer - the speaker may give one idea and then change their minds.

SPEAKING

Part 1 (2 minutes)

Select one or more questions from any of the following categories, as appropriate.

In the future

- Tell us about somewhere you'd like to visit in the future.
- What do you think you'll be doing in five years' time? (Why?)
- Is there anything you would like to learn in the future? (Why?)
- What would your ideal job be? (Why?)

Hobbies and interests

- Tell us about a particular interest or hobby you have.
- Do members of your family share your interests and hobbies? (Why / Why not?)
- Do you have the same interests now as when you were a child? (Why / Why not?)
- Do you have enough time to follow your interests? (Why / Why not?)

Shopping

- Do you spend a lot of time shopping? (Why / Why not?)
- Do you often buy things online? (Why / Why not?)
- What kind of shopping do you enjoy most? (Why?)
- Do you prefer to go shopping alone, or with friends? (Why?)

Part 2 (4 minutes)

In this part of the test you are going to have two photographs. You have to talk about your photographs on your own for about a minute, and also answer a question about your partner's photographs.

Candidate A: Here are your photographs. They show **people reading books in different situations**.

Compare the photographs, and say **why you think the people are reading books in these situations**.

Why are the people reading books in these situations?

(Candidate B), **do you use a guidebook when you visit a new place? (Why / Why not?)**

Candidate B: Here are your photographs. They show **people enjoying different holidays in the mountains**.

Compare the photographs and say **what you think the people are enjoying about their holiday in the mountains**.

> **What are the people enjoying about their holiday in the mountains?**

(Candidate A), **which of these holidays would you prefer? (Why?)**

Part 3 (4 minutes)

Now, you have to talk about something together for about two minutes.

Some people say that individuals don't do enough to look after the environment. Here are some things they think about, and a question for you to discuss.

Now talk to each other about **whether individuals do enough to look after the environment**.

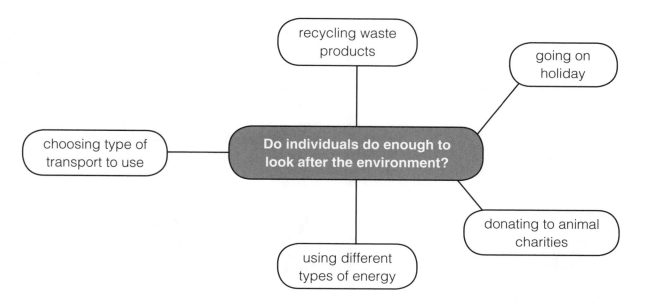

Now you have about a minute to decide which is the **most important thing individuals can do to look after the environment**.

 THINK IT THROUGH

You need to give your own opinion in Part 4. You are not graded on your views, just your language!

Part 4 (4 minutes)

Answer these questions.

- Do you think individuals can really make a big difference to the environment? (Why / Why not?)

- Do young people learn about the environment where you live? (Why / Why not?)

- Some people say it would be a good idea to encourage everyone to cycle more. Do you agree? (Why / Why not?)

- Do you think there should be more programmes on television about environmental problems? (Why / Why not?)

- Some people say there are so many environmental problems that people lose interest and don't bother to do anything. Do you agree? (Why / Why not?)

- Do you feel positive or negative about the environment in the future? (Why?)

Transcripts

Boost Your Grade

Listening (pages 10–11)

 Exercise 2b

F: Did you enjoy that programme?
M: It was a bit long, but very informative. I enjoyed finding out about environmental issues – we should know more about those.
F: I'm not sure that television is the right place for that, though it – it takes time to process complicated and important information so it's better to read books or articles. I suppose you could record the programme and watch it again, but that'd be boring.
M: I knew it'd be good – that presenter's always excellent.
F: True – but I was surprised at how fascinating it was – that sort of programme doesn't usually hold my attention.
M: You should give the next one in the series a try!

 Exercise 3b

F: Today we'll be moving on to our next important piece of work, which will be on transport problems. You'll have to do some background reading to prepare for this – now, I know you all prefer to use the internet to find information but on this occasion I want you to use your coursebooks first to get the main issues established clearly in your minds. Before I set the homework tasks, I'm going to give you back your previous assignments so you can see my comments on how you did. I have to say that I was pleasantly surprised by the quality of your writing, which isn't always up to the mark!

 Exercise 5b

M: I'm fed up with public transport in this town – the buses are never on time and they cost a fortune!
F: They're still good value when you compare them to the price of petrol. I've stopped using my car because they've reduced the number of parking spaces in the town centre and I can never find anywhere to leave it.
M: I know, I've driven round for ages just trying to find a space.
F: If they go ahead with the plan to have a pedestrian area in the town centre, I might decide to walk more – or even cycle.
M: That would give you some exercise, I suppose!

Speaking (pages 12–13)

 Exercise 5

F: Both pictures show people buying food but they are in different places. The man seems to be buying his food in a café because there are some people sitting at tables in the background, but the woman is standing outside a rather old-fashioned shop in a street where there are parked cars. In the first picture the man has just paid for his food whereas in the second picture the woman is still trying to decide what to buy, and she looks very thoughtful as she tries to make up her mind. The man is buying fast food – it looks like coffee and a muffin. On the other hand the woman is buying fruit or vegetables, which are a healthier choice. Both places seem to be fairly quiet, because there is no queue in the café and no other customers outside the shop so the woman seems to have plenty of time to choose her fruit. Both of them look unstressed and relaxed.

The people have decided to buy food in these places for different reasons. The woman may be going to do some cooking, possibly for some guests, and so she wants to buy ingredients that are fresh. She could even be deciding exactly what to cook. She might always buy her food in this shop, because she knows that the quality is good. The man is possibly in a hurry, because he's decided to take his food away – he's not going to sit down and eat it in the café. He's decided to buy his snack in this place because he knows the service is fast and perhaps he likes the coffee they make there!

Practice Test 1

Listening

 Part 1 (pages 26–27)

P: You will hear people talking in eight different situations. For questions **1–8**, choose the best answer (**A**, **B** or **C**).

1

F: We stayed at this eco resort on holiday.
M: Like an environmentally-friendly place, you mean?
F Exactly. They make all their holiday homes from recycled materials and use alternative energy – like solar panels and wind power. I wasn't sure what to expect – I suppose I thought it'd be pretty basic. It was actually really cosy with massive beds and tons of space. There was nothing much to do other than walk through pine forests, so you had to make your own entertainment. I'd expected it to be pretty quiet – we were next door to a family with a baby that kept crying, though. Anyway we still had loads of fun.

2

F: You took part in the school maths competition, didn't you?
M: I'm not sure why cos it's hardly my strongest subject. Some of the things we had to do were pretty tricky for me.
F: I coped with them pretty well. I surprised myself, to be honest. I didn't win of course – didn't even come near it. I wasn't too disappointed as the winners only got that metal award to put on the classroom wall. I'd have preferred something more useful.
M: I know what you mean. Thankfully the whole thing didn't go on all afternoon, which I thought it might.
F: Mm, at least we finished school early for the day!

3

F: Thanks for coming to this introductory talk about summer camps in America. By now you'll have accepted your offer of a place on one, so my aim today is to fill you in on who's who, where you'll be staying and so on.

Our preparation session takes place next week before you leave for camp. That'll offer you an opportunity to put your name down for the different activities available when you get there. Everyone who attends camp goes away with more confidence, new skills and having had a great time. I'm sure you've all read reviews on our website which is no doubt what encouraged you to take part!

4

M: Did you see that programme about global warming last night?
F: Yeah – I expected to hear the usual stuff about how we should be doing more to ensure the future of our planet – recycling, using sustainable energy … It always makes me feel guilty about not doing enough.
M: Right – though honestly, I can't think of much more I could personally do. Anyway it was a relief not to get a lecture about it. What they were saying about the Earth not running out of resources as quickly as they initially predicted made me think.
F: Didn't it? I might consider that in the environment essay we have to write for our science homework.

5

M: How was school?
F: OK. We talked about doing 'random acts of kindness' today.
M: What does that mean?
F: It's when you see someone who needs help and going and offering them a hand, even if you don't know them. I do my best to be like that. We discussed how it makes you feel when you do that kind of thing – whether you do it cos you genuinely want to help someone or whether you're really doing it to make yourself feel better. The conclusion we came to was that why you do something is irrelevant. The end result is the same – that the person who needs the help gets it.
M: Interesting.

6

F: I'm a university student and I've got a part-time job in a supermarket. I'm actually studying marketing, so it's provided me with some relevant experience. I've learned loads about various brands and customer loyalty – something I wouldn't have expected. I only do a few shifts at the weekends but I've been offered additional ones in the evening – I probably won't take the offer up right now as I'm so busy with my studies. I know that the job prospects are pretty good at the branch I work in though, but I'll probably go for a few marketing jobs after university first and see how I get on with that.

7

F: I'm going to do some volunteering work this summer at an elephant sanctuary where they look after African elephants that have been injured or rescued. I'll be helping out with feeding, washing them, stuff like that. I've done a load of background reading about them, I hope it'll be of some use, though it's mainly theory. I'm sure spending time with them up close will provide a totally different experience. I'm pretty open to anything they want me to get involved in. Some people aren't keen on doing the dirty jobs, but that's not an issue for me. I'm easy going so I don't expect there'll be any major problems.

8

M: Great match!
F: Wasn't it? It's really close between the teams now – every goal matters at this stage of the competition! Shame I was looking in the other direction when the goalkeeper made that save! I didn't think our team were at their best though. I'm not sure if that's anything to do with the new manager or not. And I couldn't believe there were so many spare seats – what was that all about? You'd think the stadium would've been full of people cheering the team on.
M: I know what you mean – maybe with it being such an important match they thought they'd get better coverage if they watched it on TV.

🎧 1 6 Part 2 (page 28)

P: You will hear a boy called Matt talking about an outdoor activity weekend he took part in. For questions 9–18, complete the sentences with a word or short phrase.
M: Hi, I'm Matt. I'm going to tell you about an outdoor activity weekend I went on recently, where I spent a few days learning all kinds of new stuff. I'd booked a place at the activity centre cos their website looked awesome. My uncle had taken my cousins there and they'd had a brilliant time, though it was a friend of mine who first drew my attention to it – he'd previously gone with his dad. I'm glad he did.

I'd expected to sleep in a tent when I got there – the website's full of pictures of people camping out, so when I was taken to this hut I was astonished. It was cool, though. Four of us were sharing and we got on straight away as we were walking to our introductory meeting in the shelter – that's what they called the big cabin that was at the heart of the whole place.

There were thirty of us and we were put into groups with people around the same age. We then had to come up with a name for our group. We went through loads of ideas – one guy suggested the Eagles, which I voted for, and someone else thought of Lightning, though the general preference seemed to be for the Explorers. So, that's what we went for.

Our first challenge was to make dinner. Each group had to cook for one another. None of us had a clue – I can only make simple stuff like eggs. The others had only ever made meals from packets. We were only provided with a basket of fresh vegetables – no recipes. We were a bit fed up about that but we made a soup which the others liked.

Next morning we were up early for our first activity – something called orienteering. We were driven into the woods for a few kilometres and expected to make our own way back. We had a diagram which showed major features in the landscape – no map, no compass. We had no idea where we were, so we just chose a direction and set off.

We walked through the woods, using our eyes and ears to search for clues indicating our location. When one of the boys said there was a noise like a waterfall in the background we got really excited as it was one of the things we were hoping to find… It turned out to be thunder! Eventually we came across this massive rock and knew we were heading in the right direction.

The second morning we went on a big hike. We carried water but other than that only a couple of basic tools – a knife and string. The idea was to put our survival abilities to the test. This involved making a fire without matches and a shelter from tree branches. Our group did well and I picked up a lot of useful knowledge from the tasks.

In the afternoon we took part in this game which involved climbing. You get to the top of a five-metre pole wearing a safety harness and jump off the top, aiming to hit a balloon that's hanging on a wire nearby. They told us that an alternative to the game involves grabbing a metal bar and seeing how long you can hang on!

In the evening we sat round the campfire. When our instructor got out her guitar I thought 'we're going to sing'. I wasn't exactly enthusiastic, cos my singing skills are far from polished. In fact I'd call them useless! Thankfully, the instructor sang on her own.

On the final morning, there was one last activity where we had to try something we didn't want to do. The idea was to overcome your fears. It was a good idea, though I know some people just chose activities they *wanted* to do! I went along with it, and went kayaking on the lake. I usually feel nervous on water when I can't see the bottom but I loved it! I can definitely say that the weekend was the best experience I've had.

 Part 3 (page 29)

P: You will hear five short extracts in which people are talking about women they know who inspire them. For questions **19–23**, choose from the list (**A–H**) what each speaker says about the woman who inspires them. Use the letters only once. There are three extra letters which you do not need to use.

Speaker 1

F: My grandma's the first person I go to in times of trouble. I can just pour my heart out to her about whatever problem I'm facing and she'll nod to show she knows what I'm going on about. What I most appreciate is that when I've finished, she'll somehow manage to get me to resolve the problem myself, without suggesting what I should do about it. That's a great life skill. The thing with advice is, if it's not right for you, and you don't do what someone's suggested, they don't tend to like it! She's taught me that it's better not to ask for or give it.

Speaker 2

M: My friend Florence is really inspiring. We hang out together a lot and always have a fun time. We're both into sci-fi comics and we can talk about them endlessly. She's got a medical condition which means she can't do a lot of sport or running around, which she used to love, but you'll never hear her complain. I'd like to be more like her and I always think about how she'd deal with stuff that comes up in my life. I know she'd look on the bright side of whatever it is. It's great to have a friend like that cos it makes you re-consider your own views on life.

Speaker 3

F: Whenever I go to my cousin and say 'I'm no good at this' or 'I can't do that', she just looks at me like 'Are you joking?' I don't know what she sees in me or whether she even believes what she's saying but there's no way she'll ever admit there's anything I can't do if I put my mind to it. It's nice that someone's got that amount of confidence in me. I'll always talk to her before I'm doing anything I'm a bit nervous about. When I agreed to sing in a school

concert, she was like 'Well if you can't make a good job of it, no one can!'

Speaker 4

M: I've got this really cool aunt who I spent quite a lot of time with when I was a little kid. She knew all the best games and would tell me these hilarious stories about things that had happened to her – the tears would roll down my face and I'd still be smiling hours later. I knew better than to follow any advice she gave me – it would never really be serious and she had some pretty unusual opinions about things. I don't see her as often any more cos I've moved away from our home town but if I ever need cheering up, I'll call and speak to her.

Speaker 5

F: My mum's my inspiration. She's so smart! I'm not necessarily talking about being super intelligent but having a kind of understanding of how life works. She won't hide the truth from me – if something's going to be tough, she'll let me know that. I don't always want to hear what she says but I'm always grateful in the end that she didn't try to just pretend everything was fine. She doesn't tell me what to do, though – she lets me make my own decisions. She knows you learn from your own mistakes, not from other people's. I hope I'll be as cool as Mum to my own kids one day.

 Part 4 (pages 30–31)

P: You will hear an interview with a woman called Ruth Brown, who is talking about online friendships. For questions **24–30**, choose the best answer (**A**, **B** or **C**).
M: People interact with others all over the world, through games and social media. But can these virtual connections truly compete with face-to-face friendship? We've got friendship expert Ruth Brown here with us. Ruth, how can online friendships support us?
F: Friendship's a mutual connection between people who make time to offer each other honest advice and support – why would you think friends online would be unable to fulfil that duty? Digital communication's the norm and though young people see some of their friends in person at school, they get a lot of their updates on their lives by viewing what they post online. Friends can't be with you all the time, so you don't always get guidance at the exact moment you need it. But there's nothing wrong with texting.
M: What about the things people post on social media sites?
F: Let's say you've posted something on your Facebook page or other social media site. Your friends like and share it, which boosts your mood. Based on my experience, online friendships offer a level of genuineness that face-to-face friendships don't. Because people can't see the reactions to their words, they tend to have less of a filter online – it's probable they'll express their true feelings. So you get to know them for who they really are.
M: How easy is it to make friends online?
F: The internet allows us to talk to people we want to associate with, without the need for social structures like school forcing us to fit into groups. You can find like-minded people who are into the same things as you. I'm not saying you can't have an extended social group in real life but online you can post something and potentially the people who respond will become your friends.
M: Tell us about your own online friends.

F: They mean a lot cos I'm able to express myself to people who know exactly what I'm going on about! Not that I haven't got friends away from the internet who also do, but they're not always available to chat to. Like my real-life friends, my online ones build my confidence and make me feel loved. Before I started making online friends, I didn't realise how rewarding those friendships could be.

M: Are there any drawbacks to having virtual friends?

F: You can't share experiences in the same way as you can with friends you actually see on a regular basis. Video calls aren't practical when you're out and about – you can't go to a concert with a friend online. Memories we make with friends can last a lifetime, so you're missing out on an entire chunk of history. Also, touch is important for humans and it's nice to give and receive hugs when we're feeling down. That, for me, is a crucial element of friendship and the biggest challenge to online friendships.

M: Can you ever really *know* an online friend?

F: You only know what they choose to tell you. You have to trust they are who they say they are. It pays to be a little cautious – but that's true of real-life friends, too. It's also quite one-dimensional, by which I mean it's difficult to build up a full picture of the person as you only tend to encounter them in the same social situation. Whether this matters or not is down to the individual. If you're only chatting to someone about shared musical tastes, for example, then it probably doesn't.

M: Finally, do you think we lose communication skills by spending more time online?

F: It's about as true as saying that people don't use their language skills properly when they send texts – it's incorrect as far as I'm concerned. When you can't see someone, you do miss out on visual clues as to how they're feeling, through body language and facial expression. Being able to speak confidently and maintain eye contact are important social skills, but I can't see that having a few online friends affects this negatively – as long as you have social interaction in real life too.

Boost Your Grade

Listening (pages 40–41)

 Exercise 4b

M: Hi. I'm Jack, and I'm here to talk to you all about being a stage actor. I'm sure you all think it's a glamorous job – well, I'm here to tell you it's far from what you might expect.

My first experience of the theatre came when I was at college – although my main subjects were English and maths, we all had the chance to have a go at performing arts because it was considered to be good for our personal development. That did it for me. In the beginning I got involved in the technical side of back-stage work, and I was particularly keen on doing the lighting. I did that on several college productions. Then during rehearsals for one play one of the leading actors dropped out, and I was asked to step in. Once on stage, I was hooked!

 Exercise 6

M: As a young actor you have to go to loads of auditions – after all, no-one knows who you are! I hated them – you start feeling hopeful, then you go to so many, and rarely get a job.

Lots of aspiring actors get discouraged and give up, and that's when you need a good agent to keep you going, but you must be prepared to do things you might not choose – like television advertisements. I did several, and although I didn't mind doing them I got lucky – I was spotted not by a director but by a producer and it led to my first big role on stage.

So what else is hard? It's pretty tough learning lines, and everyone has a different approach to it. I tried loads of things like reading scripts through again and again, being tested on my role by a friend, but what worked for me was recording my words and playing the tape when I went to sleep. One vital thing is not only knowing your own words, but the cues – if you don't, the performance will fail!

I'm often asked about how I build up a character I'm playing. If it's a new play the playwright is often involved but we always have meetings before we start rehearsals to discuss all the aspects of the production. They're called seminars, though I think of them more as workshops because we're building up the foundations of the production. It's crucial that our characters are real to the audience, and this means all the actors must create their characters together. When I started working with professional actors I was surprised by how seriously they took this basic preparation – I thought it would be easy for them!

Of course it's not all hard work, and we do have a lot of fun. Things can go wrong during a performance and then it's important that the audience doesn't notice. In one play I was supposed to go on stage dressed in a raincoat and boots and hand an umbrella to one of the other characters. Unfortunately it got lost backstage, so I took a hat on instead. It was a bit embarrassing, but luckily we all improvised!

People wonder why I prefer to act on stage and not in films – and film actors can certainly earn a lot of money! But there's a special kind of atmosphere in the theatre, that's created between the actors and the audience. When it works well I think of it as magic, and there's nothing quite like it.

So, are there any questions?

Speaking (pages 42–43)

 Exercises 4 and 5

M: OK, we must talk about whether it's worth spending time watching TV nowadays. Let's start with this one – hearing the news. I think it's better to find out about the news on the internet – what do you think?

F: I know what you mean – television sometimes gets the news after the internet.

M: Do you mean social media? Things like Twitter? I totally agree with you – social media is great for hearing about the news, but don't you think that it's not always accurate?

F: That's very true. At least the television broadcasts news after they've checked it, so it's more reliable.

M: Let's move on. What's your opinion about whether watching TV is fun?

F: That's a good question – some people think it is. But personally I prefer to have fun in other ways – like doing sport. People don't get enough exercise these days, and it's because they're watching television.

M: I only partly agree with you there because I like watching sport on television. I can't afford to go and watch it live.

F: In my view it's not worth watching it on television because you could have more fun getting exercise yourself instead.

M: I understand what you're saying, but you can learn a lot by watching TV documentaries – they're quite educational.

F: That's a fair point, but not all the programmes are good. I'm sorry, I still disagree with you about whether it's worth watching television.

Practice Test 2

Listening

 Part 1 (pages 56–57)

P: You will hear people talking in eight different situations. For questions **1–8**, choose the best answer (**A**, **B** or **C**).

1

M: I guess my greatest ambition is to be a scientist. I love our science lessons at school. Our teacher's so inspirational, don't you think? It must be great to have that influence on other people. I'm really into doing all the experiments, learning the theory and then seeing how it works in practice. Scientists make important contributions to the world through research. They can change things for the better. It isn't that I'm desperate to become famous or anything like that, or even necessarily to receive recognition for what I do, I just think it's cool to be able to do something that has a positive impact on society.

2

F: I love painting.

M: Me too, though I can't paint animals like you do – your wildlife pictures are incredible. I'm more into doing portraits of people.

F: Which are brilliant! When I'm painting I forget all my troubles and feel really calm, don't you?

M: I tend to feel more excited than chilled out, especially when I get something just right, though the other thing you said is true – anything I've been bothered about kind of melts away into the background. I've been experimenting with different kinds of paint recently – it takes a lot of skill to use oil paints, doesn't it?

F: Yeah, they're quite tricky to use but the effect is amazing.

3

M: Good afternoon everyone and welcome to today's basketball tournament! Play will start shortly, but I just have one or two announcements to make first. As some of you will have noticed, we've been having some repairs done to part of the roof of the sports hall, which has been damaged due to a leak. That's over in the far right-hand corner from where I'm standing now, so do stay away from any areas with tape around them. There'll be a short interval between each match, so do go along to the cafe where you'll be able to purchase refreshments – just head through the door behind me and along to the end of the corridor.

4

M: That was a neat trick!

F: Thanks! I've entered the junior championships, so I'm practising my jumps. Shame I can't get the height I've been aiming for. I'm trying to beat you!

M: I'm sure you will one day – I've been skateboarding way longer. And our local park's improved loads since they opened it – the ramps are tons better even than the big park in Mandley Village.

F: Mm, they're not up to the same standard at Mandley. Anyway, I've got to get this right cos the competition's next week and I wouldn't say I'm too confident at the moment. Hopefully I'll feel more positive once I've got this trick right.

M: You'll be great.

5

F: I've just finished Zack Hollins' new book.

M: What did you think of it?

F: I thought the overall plot was good – it didn't draw you in like the previous books in the series did, though. In the others you were on the edge of your seat, wanting to know what was going to happen next. I'm not sure why. Maybe it was something to do with the author's use of words or technique, but I still enjoyed it. There's a brand new central character, which I wasn't expecting. He was a bit weird, but you can identify with him. I guessed the ending, though it's not a disappointment. You should read it.

6

F: So, I was having a few problems with something we did in our English class and I wanted to do a bit more practice. I found this website all about grammar and my initial reaction was, 'yeah, this is going to give me all the answers I've been looking for'. Trying to navigate it wasn't exactly straightforward, though – you had to keep clicking on different links and I gave up before I found what I was looking for. It looked as though there were some fun ways to practise the grammar – like quizzes and games, but I think it's probably aimed at higher level students.

7

F: Oh, I love that song!

M: Me, too. It's the first one of hers I've actually liked – somehow you just can't get it out of your head! Song words never seem to stick in my head.

F: Yes, it's catchy. It's the tune, isn't it? I find myself whistling it in the shower or wherever I am. I think her voice is incredible, don't you?

M: I'm not a fan if I'm honest. It's really strong – I prefer softer voices personally.

F: The words make you laugh if you listen to them carefully.

M: Do you think so? I find them a bit repetitive. I like songs with messages that make you think.

8

F: I used to come out full of energy after practice, but not recently!

M: I know – and we've got a few more rehearsals to go before the performance, so I guess we'd better get used to being exhausted! It's for a few days. We'll be able to relax a bit once performances start.

F: We haven't had much praise from our director recently either. Maybe he's a bit stressed about the performances – after all, he's the director, so if people don't like it …

M: I know. He's usually pretty relaxed. Do you think he doesn't feel we're quite ready to deliver our best? He's working us hard!

F: Maybe, though I think he'd say if that was the case.

 Part 2 (page 58)

P: You will hear a girl called Joanna talking about a volunteering project she has been involved in. For questions **9–18**, complete the sentences with a word or short phrase.

F: Hey, everyone. I'm Joanna and I wanted to tell you about my recent trip to India to work on a volunteering project, which involved teaching English to young children.

My journey to India was a long one! Although I'd flown plenty of times before, I'd never travelled with an Indian airline. It was the same as any other, except that when the meals came round, most of the choices were vegetarian. That was great for me as I don't eat meat or fish.

I'd expected to have to cope with exhaustion after several hours on the plane. In fact, once I met the guy from the charity who'd come to meet me at the airport, it was just excitement that I felt. I wasn't in the least bit nervous … I wasn't in the least bit nervous about being in a place I didn't know cos the charity had prepared me well for my visit.

I'd applied to work in a rural area of India – I like peace and quiet – but nothing too remote, so I was being sent to a community in a place called Dharamsala, right up in the north of the country. Dharamsala itself is a city, and because I'd specifically requested not to be located in an urban area, I was heading to a village nearby.

We travelled by bus from the airport to the village, passing through several towns on the way. It was a fascinating journey, discovering a new culture for the first time. People were going about their daily lives, but it was very different from home. The markets in the streets were so much more colourful – I loved that – and I could see inside road-side restaurants where families were eating.

Work on the volunteer project started almost immediately – well, after a good night's sleep, that is. I stood at the front of the classroom with eager faces looking at me, ready to begin the work for the day. With an age range of between five and fourteen, the variation in English levels was what you might call dramatic. I knew I'd have to do careful planning to make sure everyone got as much as they could out of the lesson.

I wanted to get to know a little about the students, so I asked them to tell me about their likes and dislikes – in English of course. My ultimate goal was to improve their English skills in all areas – reading and writing were essential. Conversation seemed a good place to start, though, and that's what I concentrated on in the first few lessons.

I soon got into a routine, giving classes in the mornings and planning the next day's lesson in the afternoon. I was keen to make the lessons fun, so incorporated lots of games, which the students really enjoyed. It was a great way to teach things like grammar – people aren't always into having to learn all the rules, even though they need them!

As I saw the students' English improve, I had a sense of pride in what they'd achieved. They were hard-working and a joy to teach. I'd never expected them to make so much progress in such a short space of time, and it was fantastic to know they'd acquired useful skills that they could take with them through life.

When I wasn't teaching or preparing classes, I went on several amazing hilltop hikes with some of the other volunteers. I also tried yoga for the first time with my home stay family, which I enjoyed, though I failed to make any progress. I did some cooking, too – I improved a lot during my stay and can now make several delicious Indian dishes.

I was reluctant to leave my students and the family I'd stayed with at the end of my trip. Everyone had been so kind and I wanted to return their generosity in some way. So, I organised a party along with the other volunteers, where we made English food for them and they learned English songs. It was a sad goodbye, but it was the most incredible experience of my life.

 Part 3 (page 59)

P: You will hear five short extracts in which people are talking about celebrations they helped to organise. For questions **19–23**, choose from the list (**A–H**) how each speaker says they felt about the celebration. Use the letters only once. There are three extra letters which you do not need to use.

Speaker 1

M: When I graduated from college, my mum insisted on having a celebration – which I ended up having to help organise myself – cooking food and putting up decorations and so on. I'd imagined a handful of friends and family, so when on the day the doorbell kept ringing and ringing I remember thinking 'How's everyone going to fit into our tiny house?' Fortunately, the weather was good so we could use the garden. Dad gave a little speech which was embarrassing but after that I relaxed and had a pretty fun time. We'll have to do it all again next year cos my sister's finishing college then.

Speaker 2

F: My uncle retired a little while ago and my aunt wanted to hold a party for him. She asked me to get some of my friends together from dance class and do a little show. I agreed but it was a bit of a nightmare! My friends wouldn't turn up for rehearsals and one of them even got the night of the party wrong and didn't show up, so we had to manage without her. Fortunately we managed to work out new positions and stuff, though I was more nervous than I expected when my aunt announced us at the party. Thank goodness it was OK and everyone loved it.

Speaker 3

M: When my sister got married, she asked all the family to help out at the wedding. I was in charge of music which I was happy about. I asked her about the kind of stuff she wanted and then she left the rest to me. I considered playing with the band I'm in but I wasn't sure she'd be too pleased about that and anyway, I decided I'd rather enjoy the proceedings than be nervous about doing a performance. I put together this brilliant playlist which I finished the day before and I was pleased with myself cos it was a big responsibility and everyone commented on how good the music was.

Speaker 4

F: When it was my great-grandma's 90th birthday, our family decided to have a celebration for her having reached this fantastic age. She didn't want us to make a big fuss, so we called a local restaurant and booked one of their function rooms. We'd asked our cousins in Australia to come, not expecting them to cos of the long journey, so when they turned up on the day as a surprise, Grandma was over the moon, as were we. We had faith in the restaurant to put on great food and entertainment and they didn't let us down. We were really thankful for that and Grandma had a great day.

Speaker 5

M: Last year was my parents' wedding anniversary. It was a special one, so my brothers and I decided to hold a surprise party for them. We aren't natural organisers and if it hadn't been for our aunt giving us ideas of what to do and how to do it – like getting caterers in for the food – I'm not sure it would've been a success. It's a good job she was around. We invited loads of people and although not that many were able to attend, we had a fantastic time and I could tell our parents were pleased. It was hard work, though, and I wouldn't do it again!

 Part 4 (pages 60–61)

P: You will hear an interview with a psychologist called Mark Bradshaw, who is talking about how to give up bad habits. For questions **24–30**, choose the best answer (**A**, **B** or **C**).

F: We've all got bad habits and here with us today is psychologist Mark Bradshaw, who is going to tell us how to give them up. Mark, what are the most common bad habits?

M: Something I'm seeing more often is people missing meals – especially breakfast. Most people don't want to be bothered making a cooked meal at that time of day, but it's the most important meal cos it sets you up for the day – it gives you energy and helps you concentrate. It's often rushing that's the cause – you're running late cos you've overslept again, despite being so exhausted last night that you went to bed early, or whatever.

F: One of your suggestions for giving up a bad habit is to make it public.

M: OK, so you've told yourself this is the year you're going to have breakfast before leaving the house. Tell other people about what you're planning to do. Nobody wants to fail, so if you've boasted about what you're going to achieve, you'll realise you <u>have</u> to do it! You should be prepared to hear well-meaning advice you don't personally find helpful, or other people's stories about how they succeeded but only <u>you</u> can actually make it happen.

F: First of all, you have to identify your triggers, right?

M: Right. When I couldn't stop eating snacks I kept a habit record for a week – I tracked every time I reached for a snack, plus where I was and how I was feeling. This helped me spot patterns in my behaviour – perhaps I was doing it to avoid a tricky piece of work I should've been doing, for example. Looking back through my records made me go 'Oh! So <u>that's</u> what I'm doing!' It was an eye-opening exercise and one I didn't regret and thankfully I realised in time to do something about it.

F: What can you do once a bad habit's formed?

M: Once you've created a bad habit, your brain starts operating on autopilot – you keep doing it without thought. You have to get back into the driver's seat and change course. Lots of people think they can give something up without much effort and are surprised when they struggle. It's definitely achievable: if you can figure out when it is you start wasting time on the internet instead of writing your essay, for example, then that insight helps you focus on finding alternative activities during tricky moments.

F: What do you mean by 'creating obstacles'?

M: So, you know that to keep checking social media on your phone is eating up tons of time, but you can't stop doing it. Set a barrier between you and your habit. Get your parents to put your phone out of view till you've done what you need to do. Given the choice between doing something easy like checking Facebook, or something tough like math homework, we'll always take the easy route. Putting an obstacle in the way means you're more likely to get the homework done as there are no distractions.

F: What about habits like biting your nails?

M: People generally believe this is caused by feelings of anxiety, like you might experience before a stage performance and that's true in many cases. Finding something dull was my excuse – it gave me something else to do for a minute or two. People would comment and I'd feel frustrated about not being able to stop doing it. I counteracted the habit by drawing a picture on paper whenever I felt the urge to bite my nails. It worked.

F: Finally, tell us about something you call 'tapping your motivation'.

M: Let's say you're getting through several cans of cola a day – you don't stop cos you love it. One way to break the habit is using what I call a 'motivator'. This could be a picture of some jeans you're desperate for, which you hang on the fridge. This is what you'll buy with the cash you normally spend on drinks as a kind of 'well done!' to yourself. Trying to talk yourself out of a habit by saying 'I don't want bad teeth!' might seem a good idea but isn't as effective in my book.

Boost Your Grade

Listening (pages 70–71)

  Exercises 5 and 6

Speaker 1

F: I've always been keen on sport, and was good at them all but it was only recently that I decided to specialise in tennis. It was hard at first, and my parents thought I'd made the wrong decision but I was sure that it was the thing for me. I loved playing matches and taking part in competitions, and winning my first gold medal was such a highlight. The standard of the other players was very high and because it was my first major competition I couldn't have been more delighted with what I'd managed to do.

Speaker 2

M: My parents encouraged me to take up athletics, but I wasn't sure which aspect of the sport to specialise in. When I chose running I think they were proud, but worried about the huge commitment I'd have to make to be successful. I wasn't afraid of that, and put in hours of training on the road and in the gym. When I came first of course I was happy, but glad that I'd worked so hard. I wouldn't have won without that, though I suppose I must be good too!

Speaker 3

F: I love sailing, which isn't an easy sport for other people to follow – it's not like tennis where spectators sit in a stadium to watch. But like all sport, being successful brings recognition and doors open to you – you get publicity and sponsorship which make all the hard work and effort worthwhile. When I won my first race I realised this was just the start, and it was so thrilling. I don't mind the hard work, though training in the gym, is a bit boring and I do try to get out of it sometimes!

Speaker 4

M: Cycling is a hard sport – cyclists give up a lot in their lives to do all the hard physical training that's required. Races are demanding, and I was astonished at all the attention I received after I won my first gold medal – it was because I was still very young then. Having my family there was the real icing on the cake, though. Since then I've won many more but once I got a reputation people seem to expect more of me. But I love what I do, and I'll never get tired of taking part in races.

Speaker 5

M: I started playing golf as a junior when I was very young – my dad took me to the local course and I loved it from the word go. I didn't have to try very hard to start with, so I took my first medal very much in my stride, but the experience of winning made me more determined to do my best to improve no matter how difficult it may be. Now I really appreciate how important dedication is – but of course I still love playing, especially with my dad – that doesn't seem like hard work.

Speaking (pages 72–73)

 Exercise 4a

E: Do you think it's important to have a holiday every year? Why or why not?
F: I feel very strongly about that - I love holidays! I think it's important because you can relax and get away from work or college.
M: I find holidays a bit boring, to be honest!
F: Really? Could you explain what you mean?
M: Well, all my friends go away, the town is quiet and there's nothing to do.
E: Some people prefer to have one long holiday and others prefer to have several short holidays during the year. What's your opinion?
F: That's easy – I'm sure that it's one long one! Then you can really take it easy and unwind – you can travel, do loads of different stuff …
M: Sorry to interrupt, but my family like to go on short holidays – sometimes just a weekend, and it breaks the year up very well. It seems to me that's a better way of having holidays.

Practice Test 3

Listening

 Part 1 (pages 86–87)

P: You will hear people talking in eight different situations. For questions **1–8,** choose the best answer (**A**, **B** or **C**).

1

F: I'm enjoying our music classes, are you?
M: Yeah, I am, actually. I mean, I've never done anything like composition before. I wouldn't exactly call it fun, though it's quite satisfying when you manage to complete a piece.
F: I'm not very imaginative, so I don't think it's my thing at all, especially cos I don't play any instruments. What I <u>do</u> like is learning about different historical periods of music – hearing stuff I've never heard before.
M: Oh, I know what you mean – that early 20th century stuff's my favourite. I'd love to learn the trumpet – not sure I'd be any good at it, though!
F: I don't see why not.

2

F: You're into snowboarding, aren't you?
M: Yeah – I've been doing it since I was a kid. I'm pretty speedy downhill, though I hardly ever get down Black Mountain without falling over. My goal is to get down there faster than ever before – that's what I get a real sense of excitement from. Some of the jumps on the way down are a challenge but I'm getting there. My instructor's putting me in for the senior competition cos I've improved a lot. I won the junior freestyle contest last year but I was so nervous beforehand – I don't know how much fun competing really is. Maybe it's worth it to win, though.

3

F: I've been making jewellery – earrings, necklaces, stuff like that – for a couple of years now. I make things I'd like to wear – it stops me spending hours staring in shop windows, wishing I could have this, that or the other. I have quite a specific style, which some people like and some don't. That's irrelevant to me cos I'm going to wear it anyway. It's tricky dealing with such tiny pieces of metal or beads but it's something I'm driven to do – I have all these ideas in my head and I just have to do something about it. I might go on to do a jewellery design course at some point.

4

M: There's nothing like planning when you're thinking of writing a story. The more you plan, the easier it will be when you actually start the writing process. At this point you need to think about developing your characters – they need to be realistic or your readers won't be able to identify with them and might lose interest. Include dialogue and remember – something's got to happen in the story. We've all read loads of books which don't seem to go anywhere or have no aim and you end up thinking – what was the point of reading that? Once you do start writing, make sure your opening paragraph really draws readers in.

5

M: Oh, you read that music magazine, too. What do you think about it?
F: It's cool. I get it whenever I can and don't usually miss an issue when something comes with it – like last month, they gave away those vouchers.
M: Oh, I missed out on them! There's a lot of wasted space – all those pictures and not enough to read …
F: … and it's quite a thin magazine compared to some of the others. The question and answer sessions they print with musicians are what I like best – why don't they ever get the big stars, though? Maybe they're more difficult to get hold of or too expensive or something.
M: I guess.

6

F: How's the job at the furniture store going?
M: It's OK. I'm working in the warehouse and I've been learning how all the machinery works – when furniture's delivered, they have this amazing automatic system where it gets stacked on shelves. There's tons to get my head round, so I'm still picking things up, but everyone's patient and friendly. I didn't think some of the more experienced people would be interested in me but they are. Most people have been there years, so I guess that says something about how good it is to work there – like you get plenty of breaks, the pay's decent, all that stuff. I like it.

7

M: This week we're starting our 'dark nights' project. We're going into the countryside where there's no light pollution to make a map of the stars we see – you'll be amazed by what's there if you haven't seen it before. There's going to be a 'super moon' on Thursday, which is when the full moon is closer to the Earth than usual. It'll look bigger than it normally does – it's OK to look at it, unlike the sun. Most of you have returned your contact details form which we need in case of emergency. I need the rest of them by tomorrow or you won't be able to come with us.

8

F: Are you still going to Matt's party on Saturday?
M: Yeah, you?
F: Yeah. It's a barbecue, isn't it? I've never been to one in this country before – is it usual to go along with your own food?
M: Only if you have a special diet or something, like you're vegetarian or whatever.
F: Didn't you say I could get a lift there with you and your brother?
M: Actually I think we'll have go on to the bus now cos he's working that afternoon – he'll pick us up later, though, and drop you at home.
F: As long as it isn't too late. I've got to finish that art project for college on Sunday.
M: So have I.

 Part 2 (page 88)

P: You will hear a young woman called Steffi talking about doing a walk in the mountains. For questions 9–18, complete the sentences with a word or short phrase.

F: My name's Steffi and last month I went on a really interesting walk in the hills of the mountain district near where I live. The route we took is known as the 'Iron Way' and it was pretty adventurous, let me tell you. I'd done the White Peak walk before, but this was truly incredible!

What was so good about it? Well, there are loads of these routes through mountains and they make use of different features, such as bridges which seem to be suspended mid-air and wooden walkways. There are steel cables which you grab onto for safety, too. It's really exciting stuff!

This allows people with not much climbing experience to go along routes that ordinarily only climbers can do and it's a fantastic way to experience the views. They are as spectacular as people say but you only get to see them when you're up in the rocky bits at the top of the mountains.

We started off at the office at the bottom of the climb, where we met our guide. He went through all the health and safety stuff and gave us the equipment we'd need. That included a harness – that's the thing that connects you to a rope for safety purposes. I had a helmet already, so I didn't need to borrow that.

As we headed up the mountain, our guide told us about a few things we should look out for along the way. He said we'd be stopping at a magnificent waterfall for photos, though if we wanted to see wildlife we'd have to look a bit harder. Visitors used to be on the watch for eagles but there are none left now. We spotted goats high up on a cliff, though. They looked really cute cos they were so small.

The walk got gradually steeper until we had to use ladders attached to the rock face. That's when I felt grateful for being as fit as I was but still very dizzy! I didn't dare look down – the ground seemed so far away. Thankfully it didn't last long and I was soon in awe of how tiny everything looked below us.

We stopped for lunch before the scariest part of the climb, which involved moving along a narrow ledge only a few centimetres wide. We had to press our bodies against the rock. It seemed risky, but because of all our safety equipment, we were really in no harm at all. I was still relieved when we got to the end though!

Thankfully after this the walk was gentler and we had more time to look around us. Our guide pointed out geographical features, such as the shape of the valley which had been carved out by ice thousands of years ago. There were also some huge boulders – massive rocks standing on end like giants. They were impressive, even from a distance.

You would have thought that coming down the mountain would have been easier than climbing up it. Well, it wasn't! We had to do something called abseiling, which is where you descend the rock on a rope. You have to sort of lean backwards over the edge of a cliff and walk down it facing the rock. I'd never done it before, so I was incredibly proud of myself for being brave enough to do it!

There are lots of these routes all over the world and they have some amazing things to see. There's one that goes along a glacier in Switzerland which looks stunning. One in Kenya that includes a safari – the animals are in the same park as the mountains – that's top of my list if I can ever afford to get there. Then there's one in Peru where you stay in a kind of glass bubble hanging over the edge – I'd be way too scared to do that!

Part 3 (page 89)

P: You will hear five short extracts in which people are talking about their ambitions. For questions **19–23**, choose from the list **(A–H)** what each speaker says about why they want to achieve their ambition. Use the letters only once. There are three extra letters which you do not need to use.

Speaker 1

F: Becoming a professional dancer's my number one ambition. Whether I'll achieve that or not, I don't know but I'm going to do my best. I started dancing when I was four and I haven't stopped since. I used to beg my mum to take me to watch ballets at the theatre and I'd sit in awe at what the dancers could do. Now I'm going to find out what I'm capable of. How far can I go? How far can my body go? If I don't ever get to be on stage in a professional performance then so be it – at least I'll be confident I did everything I could've done.

Speaker 2

M: Whenever I tell anyone I'm going to be in a rock band, they kind of roll their eyes like 'Yeah, that's what every young guy wants to do!' I've never actually said that the band'll be hugely successful and get worldwide recognition, or earn a ton of money. I know I'm not that good on the guitar and never will be. That doesn't mean I can't have a brilliant time messing about with my mates, having a laugh. Isn't that what life's all about? At the moment I'm trying to find people to join me – I've found a drummer, so we just need a singer to complete the band.

Speaker 3

F: Climb Mount Everest. That's my ambition. I've wanted to do that for as long as I can remember. I'm not sure anyone takes me seriously, even though I've been making huge progress in my climbing lessons. I'm going to show them, just you wait and see. I've been reading this autobiography of a guy who's pretty well-known in the climbing world and he's climbed Everest twice – imagine! So many people do it these days, you never even hear about them – it isn't front-page news anymore and they aren't interviewed for magazines. I wouldn't be doing it for that reason anyway. All I can say is, watch this space.

Speaker 4

M: What's my greatest ambition? Good question! I think doing a sky-dive is at the top of my list. You know, where you jump out of a plane and parachute down? Would I be scared? You bet I would! But imagine how amazing you'd feel when you'd finished, especially if you'd raised a ton of money for charity – that's the reason I'd even consider doing it. I just want to contribute something to society, however small. I haven't actually organised the jump yet, but a few of us are going to do the training soon – and after that it will all start to become a reality!

Speaker 5

F: Since we went to Spain on holiday, all I've ever wanted to do is see the world. I can't get enough of new places, new people, new cultures. They say that travel broadens the mind and I always wondered what that meant. I think it's getting a new perspective on things, isn't it? You know, like maybe people in other places have different ways of doing things – maybe better ways of doing things. When I

finish college, before I go to university I want to do a gap year where I go backpacking round South America. I'm going to write a blog – hopefully people will want to read it!

 Part 4 (pages 90–91)

P: You will hear an interview with a woman called Carly Smith, who is talking about taking part in a TV talent competition. For questions **24–30**, choose the best answer (**A**, **B** or **C**).

M: Today, we're talking to Carly Smith, who took part in a TV talent competition, taking place over several weeks. Carly, tell us about applying for the competition.

F: I saw an advert about applying and thought, why not give it a go? I've done acrobatics since I was a kid – which is like gymnastics, except it doesn't rely on equipment and is more about performance. I love it! The TV competition took place over three weeks and each week, judges voted for participants and someone got knocked out. I hadn't paid a lot of attention to that before so I'm not sure why it suddenly appealed to me but it seemed like a thrilling thing to get involved in.

M: Did you have to do an audition?

F: Yeah – you've got to prove you can actually <u>do</u> something before you get a place in the competition. I stood in front of the judges and I remember thinking 'Please don't let me make any mistakes!' I did – but I hoped the judges hadn't noticed them. It was impossible to know from their expressions how much they'd enjoyed what I'd done, so all I could do was wait to find out whether I'd got through to the next stage.

M: You were successful! What happened next?

F: I had a month before the live shows started. That sounds like a long time but I knew if I was too relaxed about it, I wouldn't be well-enough prepared. I thought, right, I'd better get practising! I'd found out that there was another local acrobatic group taking part, so I desperately wanted to do better than them. I focused on making my performance unusual – throwing in some unexpected moves and making it fun. People say when you're in a competition you should imagine yourself winning – but I didn't because that wasn't necessarily my goal.

M: What was the first live show like?

F: I'd never been in a TV studio and I found the whole thing fascinating. Each performer was given a three-minute slot to practise in the performance area and that's when what I was about to do hit me. I wasn't just going to have a TV camera in my face but an audience in the studio, too. What if they put me off? My major concern was that the floor was really smooth – what if I slipped? Thankfully everything went well.

M: How did it feel waiting for the judges to vote on putting you through to the next stage?

F: Awful! Although I hadn't watched the other participants during their live performance, I'd seen them during practice and knew that the standards were incredibly high. As we all stood in front of the judges, I'd sort of accepted that there was no way I could compare favourably to some of the others. Everything had gone according to plan in my performance, though, and there was nothing I could do to influence their decision.

M: How did it feel when you were put through to the second live show?

F: I'd put so much energy into that first performance and then I suddenly thought I'm going to have to do something different now. I hadn't thought that far ahead.

So, although on the one hand I was delighted to have got through, another part of me briefly wondered how I was going to carry on. I never seriously considered quitting, but as there was only a week to prepare this time, I knew I'd better get my ideas together quickly.
M: And you made it through to the final.
F: Yes, that was the third and last show. I don't remember ever having felt so nervous. My final performance went well – in fact it's probably the best one I've ever done, thanks to all the practice and new stuff I'd learned. I won't say I didn't regret that it was the end of the adventure, but it had been challenging too. I came second, which was brilliant. All the participants had a party after the show and then we went our separate ways as if we'd never met!

Practice Test 4

Listening

 Part 1 (pages 108–109)

P: You will hear people talking in eight different situations. For questions **1–8,** choose the best answer (**A**, **B** or **C**).

1

F: You play keyboards, don't you?
M: I'm learning. I had this idea I'd join a band. I doubt I'll ever be good enough – my progress hasn't been the fastest.
F: I heard that if you've ever learned an instrument, it's really good for your brain as you get older.
M: That's good to know. Anyway, how are you getting on with the drums?
F: Same as you – it's far trickier than I expected it to be. Maybe we should have started learning when we were younger. I don't find all the practice particularly exciting.
M: It'll be worth it when we can play fun stuff rather than just learning the notes.
F: Can't wait!

2

F: What did you do in the school holidays?
M: Oh, we went camping in the mountains. I hadn't even put a tent up before so I practised with Dad in the garden and it went smoothly when we got there. We stayed in this forest. We'd decided to have our own adventure rather than just go to an existing campsite. I was a bit uneasy cos I'd heard about these wildcats that live there. I discovered they're no danger to humans, though, and we didn't spot any anyway. I thought we were going to just have a chilled out time – actually it was action-packed – we went swimming, fishing, you name it!

3

M: This is an announcement for all passengers on platform six. We would like to apologise for the late running of the 17.22 service to Chessel. This is due to an earlier signal failure on the line. The train is running approximately 30 – that's three, zero – minutes late and will now leave from platform four. Unfortunately, the service will not stop at Baiton this evening and any passengers wishing to travel to this stop should disembark at Borley and catch the 19.03 service to Henton.

Passengers requiring any further information about this evening's services should proceed to the customer service desk. Thank you for your attention.

4

M: I'm learning to sing.
F: Cool! Are you having lessons?
M: Yeah. I had the first one on Monday. I wasn't sure whether I would have a good enough singing voice. When I got there, the teacher convinced me that it's more about enjoyment than anything. I have no intention of being a professional anyway! That's probably a good thing cos I'm not sure I'll ever get my head round the music – I couldn't see how what it said on the page was anything to do with the sound I was trying to make!
F: What songs did you sing?
M: Nothing I recognised – though hopefully we'll do some stuff I know in the future.

5

M: Are you playing that game *again*? Don't you ever get bored with it?
F: Never!
M: What, even though you just keep doing the same thing over and over? I thought it was brilliant at first, good fun and everything – it's a bit repetitive though.
F: Actually, you never do the same thing twice and it keeps your brain active!
M: I suppose you do need to think carefully about what you're doing, especially at that speed. You can't take your eyes off the screen for a second. It's hard to keep that up over the whole game. And then when you can't complete a level and you have to start all over again, it's frustrating!

6

F: Everyone assumes climbing one of the highest peaks in the world was something I'd always set out to do. Nothing could be further from the truth. A friend convinced me to do it in order to raise money for charity. Eventually, after a lot of training, we set off. I nearly turned back a couple of times but I had a lot of support and encouragement from my instructor and eventually we reached the top. I was immensely proud of having managed to go from never having climbed to having got up there. The only downside was the cloud cover which meant we couldn't see very far. Apparently it's stunning.

7

F: Hey, Mel! It's me. Listen, it's John's surprise birthday party on Saturday. Are you still going? I hope so. Anyway, if you are, I wondered whether you'd consider giving a bit of a speech. You're his best friend and I thought you must have some funny stories to share from when you were at school. It's fine if you don't fancy it – I might be able to ask Pete to do it instead. Anyway, I've decided to go ahead with the barbecue after all – I know I said I might get outside caterers to do some sandwiches but I'm sticking with the plan. Anyway, let me know.

8

F: Have you been to that new café in town?
M: Yeah. I liked it. The menu was pretty much as I thought it would be – pizzas, burgers – nothing that exciting but it was still decent. They'd advertised a gaming lounge which I thought sounded brilliant. It's a shame it wasn't set up when I went, though. Hopefully it'll be ready soon cos

it'll be brilliant getting served while you play. There were loads of people our age there, though – I had a real laugh with some mates from college. It's great to have a place of our own where we can hang out, isn't it?

F: Yeah, I know!

 Part 2 (page 110)

P: You will hear a boy called Olly talking about setting up a band. For questions 9–18, complete the sentences with a word or short phrase.

M: I'm Olly and I thought I'd share my experience with you about playing guitar in a band. I started playing the instrument when I was about eight. I wouldn't say I was exactly what you'd call keen to do the classes – but my dad regretted never having taken up the offer of music lessons when he was a kid so he thought it'd be good for me to have a go. I loved it straightaway.

It was never any problem doing my practice – I knew other kids who hated it. I'd spend hours learning new pieces, listening to stuff on the internet. I ordered a ton of music to learn – sometimes it was way above my level but I liked the challenge. I think my parents actually missed me sometimes cos I was so into what I was doing I spent hardly any of my free time with them!

After a few years of that I reckoned it'd be good to start playing with other musicians. There was an orchestra at school – they had no need for guitars, though, and the only thing that seemed to be available in the town I grew up in was a folk group, which didn't really appeal. Rock music was what I was into – not that.

So, I decided to set my own band up. I asked my music teacher at school how I could advertise and she let me put a sign up on the school noticeboard. The only people who got in touch were other guitar players, so I had to consider putting an ad elsewhere – like a website. That did the trick and I managed to find a drummer and a singer.

Our main problem was where to practise. We didn't all go to the same school, so the music rooms there weren't an option. Our bedrooms seemed the best idea, though they turned out to be inconvenient, and renting a studio space was way too expensive. In the end the drummer's parents said we could use their basement. We're still there – it's a cool space.

Luckily we all get on as a group, so there's no tension. Our musical influences are similar, so we generally agree on the kind of stuff we play. The only thing we fell out about was what to call ourselves. Jen, the singer, wanted Black Butterfly, whereas Danny – he's the drummer – thought of Motor Mouth. I came up with Red Mist which is what we went for in the end.

We aren't much good at songwriting! We all had a go but nothing seemed to work. So the first things we played weren't our own songs but what they call cover songs – you know, famous stuff that we'd learned to play ourselves. Our drummer's brother's pretty good at coming up with lyrics, so he writes our songs now and we come up with the tunes.

We played our first gig six months ago. It wasn't at a theatre or concert venue like we'd hoped but a festival. We did an audition and they loved us. We were on last and thought most people would've gone home by then, but it was still crowded. It all went pretty well.

People who saw us perform that night asked for our contact details and we've been getting bookings ever since. We've done a birthday party, a barbecue, which was great fun … the ultimate concert for me, though, was a wedding! I bet you'd never have guessed that cos you wouldn't expect a rock band to do that kind of thing. Everyone got up and danced and it was great to play a part in someone's special day.

People keep asking us if we've got a manager but so far we've sorted everything out ourselves. We're not that big and we haven't recorded anything yet. Plus, we don't get paid – though that's something we're thinking about changing. A music agent would be helpful if we want to make it big – so we're looking into that at the moment. I'm really excited about our future!

 Part 3 (page 111)

P: You will hear five short extracts in which people are talking about holidays they have been on. For questions **19–23**, choose from the list (**A–H**) what each speaker says they enjoyed most about the holiday. Use the letters only once. There are three extra letters which you do not need to use.

Speaker 1

M: I went to Spain with my family last year. It was brilliant – we stayed in this fantastic apartment right by the sea. I'd done Spanish at school but never had the chance to try out any of the words with native speakers. I got chatting to a boy called Pablo who was about my age and I was totally amazed when he got what I was saying – not that I understood everything he said back. I think the thing that made me go 'Wow!', was learning about the way of life there. I hadn't considered how different the customs and traditions might be. I'm staying with Pablo's family next summer. Can't wait!

Speaker 2

F: I've always been big on finding out about different cultures and their past, which is precisely why I went on a Nile Cruise in Egypt with a study group. Everything was just as fascinating as I'd expected it to be, though the real highlight of the trip was something else entirely. Of course, the temples and other sites were truly incredible but it hadn't crossed my mind that I'd get the chance to socialise – I thought we'd just be spending time in our own little group, so it was a nice surprise to have that element of the trip as well. I even went to a local family's home for dinner.

Speaker 3

M: One of my best holidays was when I went to Thailand a couple of years ago with my wife. I rarely get time away from my hectic work schedule so I was really looking forward to just chilling out for a couple of weeks. That wasn't to be – although the resort itself was peaceful and away from all the sights of the cities, there were a ton of things to get involved in and that's where I scuba dived for the first time. I haven't stopped since. We're going back to Thailand for our wedding anniversary in a few months' time and doing a cookery course – we love Thai dishes.

Speaker 4

F: I couldn't wait to go away with some of my girlfriends after university and we organised a trip to Italy. I think we came to that decision cos we're all really into the cuisine – it's delicious. If we'd done any research in advance about Rome, we'd have realised just what a historical place we were going to. None of us knew much about Roman emperors or anything. The sites were awesome though! We spent days wandering around with our mouths open in shock. I would definitely go back – we had an amazing time and it was made all the better by the surprise of it all.

Speaker 5

M: Mum and Dad dragged my brother and me to Greece last year on a so-called 'history trip'. The things we saw were actually much more fascinating than I thought they would be, so that was an unexpected bonus. I didn't pay a lot of attention to the facts – I'm more of a visual person really. What got me was seeing the Greek alphabet everywhere – I spent ages trying to interpret what the letters stood for. It looked so different, yet some things were recognisable when you'd worked out the sounds. My brother and I spent ages doing that – it was a real laugh and turned the holiday into a brilliant one.

Part 4 (pages 112–113)

P: You will hear an interview with a young woman called Emma Holloway, who writes a blog. For questions **24–30**, choose the best answer (**A**, **B** or **C**).

M: Emma Holloway is a successful blogger. Emma, how did it all begin?

F: Well, it was during one of my school holidays when I spotted a gap in what was out there. There were loads of blogs that seemed to target either gender, but I wanted to do something that would involve all of us. I'm not saying they weren't any good – some of them are fascinating to read and the writing style's impressive. But I wanted to cover a variety of topics – there are loads of fashion and music blogs and not much else.

M: How did you get people interested in reading your blog?

F: At first I was a bit unsure about whether or not I was choosing the right topics and I only shared what I was doing with a few close friends and family members, not expecting it to take off at all. They loved it and my friends ended up telling other mates and out of the blue this teen magazine got interested in what I was doing and included a link from their online magazine – I couldn't even have imagined something like that happening! I've got a decent following now which is really beyond my wildest dreams.

M: Have you ever come into contact with any of your readers?

F: Apart from friends my readers are all over the place, so meeting any of them wasn't anything I ever expected to happen. I was in London one day on the underground and I heard this girl talking about some article she'd read and it slowly came to me that it was my blog she was talking about! I sat there petrified that she'd criticise something. Then she got off and I wondered if I'd missed an opportunity to learn more about my readers.

M: Where do you get your inspiration from?

F: About what to write about, you mean? I like to talk about ideas as much as anything – so, not just stuff I've seen and done. I keep my eyes and ears open at all times in case something interesting comes to my attention. I'm

an avid reader – that helps me put sentences together better and has really built up my vocabulary. It's when I'm sitting on the bus or wherever and bits of people's conversations drift my way that my brain starts ticking and the creativity starts flowing.

M: Tell us a bit more about how you write.

F: I write about topics which are typically of interest to people my age – I'm not saying anything I come up with is particularly original. I'm not giving advice or suggesting how people should live their lives or anything like that. What I think is crucial to success is that people know I'm just like them – that's what makes readers keep coming back.

M: Have you given any thought to your future career?

F: I get asked all the time whether I want to be a professional writer. Nothing could be further from the truth. I love science and I think I'd quite like to go into research – so the only connection to writing would be if I wrote scientific papers – but if that doesn't happen I won't be bothered about it – either the writing or that job. There's still time to think about it. Maybe I'll get tired of having to come up with things to write about in my blog. What will be, will be! I'll just keep going, keep studying and see what happens.

M: Finally, have you got any advice for people who might like to write a blog themselves?

F: It can be tempting to air your opinions about things you have little experience of. I'd say avoid that – stick to what you know, what you feel passionate about and do your research if you aren't sure of the facts. It's important to work on your writing style. There's no need to get all bothered about the occasional spelling mistake – the message is more important. And … don't worry if it takes a while to get readers, just keep going!

Answers

Boost Your Grade

Reading and Use of English (pages 6–7)

1 1 c 2 f 3 g 4 i 5 d 6 h 7 e
       8 b 9 k 10 l 11 j 12 a

2 **b)** Mary never turns up on time – it's so annoying!
       c) Did you hear that John's parents allowed him to drive the family car?
       d) 'I advise you to do your homework more carefully!' said the teacher.
       e) It's possible that I can't come to your party – I'll have to let you know.
       f) I regret that I didn't study harder last year!

3a Sentences 1 and 5

4 **a)** 2 It should be 'you had not recommended it'.
       b) 8 It should be 'wishes'.
       c) 3 It should be 'suggested going out'.
       d) 7 It should be 'to <u>make</u> a decision'.
       e) 6 It should be 'succeed'.
       f) 4 It should be 'have forgotten to turn '.

Boost Your Grade

Writing (pages 8–9)

1 Statement b: An essay should be written in a formal style as it presents an academic argument or point of view.

2 **a)** Yes
       Possible answers:
       b) New experiences: students often stay in their own town when they are young and at school. Travel helps them see the world and become independent. Learning languages is useful in a global world.

3 Idea a: The two notes (1 and 2) in the task support the statement. Ideas b and c also support the idea, so it is good to include Idea a which opposes it. One example could be that students need to have saved money when they go to university.

4 **A**: It introduces the topic without giving the writer's point of view. A rhetorical question is a good way to start any essay.

5 1 Firstly 2 also 3 Secondly 4 After all
       5 On the other hand 6 For this reason 7 although

6 **B**: It sums up the ideas in the essay and comes to a logical conclusion which gives the writer's opinion.

7 1 Introduction 2 First given idea (for)
       3 Second given idea (for) 4 Third own idea (against)
       5 conclusion

8 & 9 Students' own answers

Boost Your Grade

Listening (pages 10–11)

1 **a)** emotion **b)** opinion/attitude **c)** topic
       d) agreement **e)** detail **f)** attitude/opinion
       g) detail **h)** topic **i)** agreement
       j) purpose in speaking

2a Attitude/opinion

2b A

2c
       F: Did you enjoy that programme?
       M: It was a bit long, but very informative. I enjoyed finding out about environmental issues – we should know more about those.
       F: I'm not sure that television is the right place for that, though it – takes time to process complicated and important information so it's better to read books or articles. I suppose you could record the programme and watch it again, but that'd be boring.
       M: I knew it'd be good – that presenter's always excellent.
       F: True – <u>but I was surprised at how fascinating it was – that sort of programme doesn't usually hold my attention</u>.
       M: You should give the next one in the series a try!

3a Purpose

3b C

3c
       F: Today we'll be moving on to our next important piece of work, which will be on transport problems. You'll have to do some background reading to prepare for this – now, I know you all prefer to use the internet to find information <u>but on this occasion</u>

I want you to use your coursebooks first to get the main issues established clearly in your minds. Before I set the homework tasks I'm going to give you back your previous assignments so you can see my comments on how you did. I have to say that I was pleasantly surprised by the quality of your writing, which isn't always up to the mark!

4   **a)** disagree   **b)** agree   **c)** agree   **d)** disagree
       e) disagree   **f)** agree

5b   B

5c   📄

M: I'm fed up with public transport in this town – the buses are never on time and they cost a fortune!
F: They're still good value when you compare them to the price of petrol. I've stopped using my car because they've reduced the number of parking spaces in the town centre and I can never find anywhere to leave it.
M: I know, I've driven round for ages just trying to find a space.
F: If they go ahead with the plan to have a pedestrian area in the town centre I might decide to walk more – or even cycle.
M: That would give you some exercise, I suppose!

Boost Your Grade

Speaking (pages 12–13)

1   b and d

2a   **a)** He   **b)** She   **c)** She   **d)** He   **e)** He   **f)** She   **g)** Both

2b   Students' own answers

2c   Possible answers:
Although the woman is buying healthy food from a local shop, the man is buying a snack in a café. Both people seem to be unstressed and relaxed.

3   Possible answers:
a) supermarket/market/discount store/specialist shop/shopping mall
b) more choice/cheaper prices/convenience/buying something special

4   Possible answers:
The man is in a hurry/he's having a break from work
The woman is cooking a special meal/she wants to buy good quality ingredients

5   b

6   Reasons a and b

Practice Test 1

Reading and Use of English (pages 14–23)

Part 1 (page 14)

1 C   **2** B   **3** C   **4** A   **5** C   **6** B   **7** B   **8** D

Part 2 (page 15)

9 last   **10** took   **11** as   **12** after   **13** on   **14** During   **15** give   **16** had

Part 3 (page 16)

17 wealthy   **18** increasingly   **19** competition   **20** comparable   **21** accommodation   **22** additional   **23** understandable   **24** retirement

Part 4 (page 17)

25 they are supposed to   **26** we have to   **27** unless we leave   **28** can't / cannot stand waiting   **29** aren't enough   **30** insisted on finishing the game

Part 5 (pages 18–19)

31 C   **32** D   **33** A   **34** B   **35** D   **36** B

Part 6 (pages 20–21)

37 F   **38** D   **39** A   **40** E   **41** G   **42** C

Boost your grade! (page 21)

1   Students' own answers

2   Paragraph 1 c
       Paragraph 2 f
       Paragraph 3 e
       Paragraph 4 b
       Paragraph 5 a
       Paragraph 6 d

3a   **a)** Sentence G
        c) Sentence F
        e) Sentence A
        f) Sentence D

Part 7 (pages 22–23)
43 D   **44** B   **45** D   **46** C   **47** A   **48** B   **49** A   **50** B   **51** C   **52** A

Boost your grade! (page 22)

a) fantastic **b)** incredible **c)** a bonus **d)** remember
e) not realise

Writing (pages 24–25)

Sample answers

Part 1 (page 24)

Many people worry about the number of endangered animals there are in the wild and want to save them. However, is this really important in today's world?

Firstly, it is difficult to get accurate numbers of endangered animals, and even more difficult to work out practical ways of saving them. There are difficulties such as whether you bring them into a controlled situation like a zoo, which is unnatural, or try to protect them in the wild, which is a challenge.

What's more, there is the cost involved. It is very expensive to protect animals and it's hard to justify using money that could help people instead. There are animal charities which raise money to save endangered animals, but maybe it is better to spend the money on helping animals we use, like horses or donkeys.

Finally there is the question of whether we should try to save endangered species at all. Some species die out naturally as part of the circle of life. Should we interfere with this?

On balance, people want to save endangered wild animals to preserve them for future generations, and this may be vital.

189 words

Part 2 (page 25)

2

Holidays are great – we all love getting away from it all and taking it easy or exploring new places. I've enjoyed all my holidays, but one in particular was very special.

It was one summer when I went on an adventure holiday in the mountains with a group of friends. I had never been to the mountains before, and the scenery was spectacular. We tried lots of sports I had only dreamed of, like kayaking, white water rafting and rock climbing. I learned so many new things and was able to challenge myself physically.

What made it the best holiday I have ever had was my friends. We spent the evenings together talking about the adventures of the day and sharing our funny experiences. We laughed so much when one friend described the way he fell out of his kayak and had to be rescued.

So that's why it was my best holiday ever – and it shows that the people you share your holiday with are as important as the place you visit or the things you do.

178 words

Part 2 (page 25)

3

Hi Jo,

I'm sorry I haven't emailed for a while but I've been really busy moving in to my new house.

Everything's going really well and I love the house. It hasn't taken long to feel completely at home. It's bigger than the old house, so we've got more space for all our things. It's more modern, too, as it was only built last year. I've got my own room, which means I can play my music whenever I want without my sister complaining about it! That's a real bonus! One disadvantage is the garden is quite small, but I don't mind that – it's still big enough to have a barbecue in the summer!

There are loads of things to do in this part of town. There are two parks nearby where I can go jogging and a really good swimming pool which is only a bus-ride away. It's a pity that it's a long walk to the cinema, but there are so many other advantages rhat it doesn't really matter.

Why don't you come and visit next Saturday? I can show you everything!

Love,

185 words

Part 2 (page 25)

4

Visit to the museum

Introduction

The aim of this report is to give information about my recent visit to a new local history museum in the town, to assess its success and to make recommendations about visiting it.

Information about the museum

The museum focuses on local history, and contains a number of objects that were discovered when a new block of flats was being built in the town. These objects include pottery and tools from hundreds of years ago. They are displayed in a very imaginative way and it is possible to rent an audio guide which really brings the past to life although I didn't have time to rent it. There are also models of the town showing how it has changed over the years, which are fascinating.

I would have liked more written information everywhere in the museum, as it was necessary to rent the audio guide to understand everything.

Recommendations

The museum is worth visiting as it gives a different view of our town. I recommend:
- leaving enough time to rent the audio guide
- taking time to study the models of the town

185 words

Listening (pages 26–31)

Part 1 (pages 26–27)

1 C **2** B **3** C **4** A **5** B **6** C **7** B **8** A

Part 2 (page 28)

9 friend **10** hut **11** Explorers **12** recipes **13** diagram **14** waterfall **15** survival **16** balloon **17** useless **18** fears

Part 3 (page 29)

19 E **20** H **21** D **22** G **23** F

Part 4 (pages 30–31)

24 C **25** A **26** B **27** A **28** B **29** C **30** A

Boost your grade! (page 31)

1   c

2   **difficult:** Listen to see if Ruth says something about the problems of giving advice on social media.

more: She might compare the amount of contact people have online and face-to-face.

as satisfying as: She might explain that both types of friendship are equally important.

Boost Your Grade

Reading and Use of English (pages 36–37)

2a   **1** c **2** e **3** d **4** f **5** a **6** b

2   I love travelling with <u>friends</u>. <u>They</u> make a trip fun when we're together.

3   You can <u>get information</u> in <u>different ways</u>. One of <u>these</u> is the internet.

4   It's good to check with <u>travel agents</u> about <u>flights</u>. <u>They</u> give useful information about <u>them</u>.

5   There's often a <u>tour guide</u> at historical sites. If <u>so</u>, you can ask <u>him or her</u> questions.

6   <u>Travel</u> can be <u>expensive</u>. <u>This means</u> many people choose to stay at home.

2b   **e)** *They* refers to friends.
d) *these* refers to ways of finding information
f) *They* refers to travel agents and *them* refers to flights.
a) *so* refers to whether there is a tour guide at the site and *him* or *her* refers to a tour guide.
b) *This means* refers to travel is expensive.

3   **a)** they **b)** them **c)** this **d)** it **e)** they're **f)** it's

4   1 G 2 C 3 A 4 F 5 B 6 D

Boost Your Grade

Writing (pages 38–39)

1   The correct statements are a, c, d and f.

3   Suggestions: the kind of holiday you enjoy and the reasons; what is most enjoyable about having a holiday at all

4a   Paragraph b – reason 2. The paragraph engages the reader by saying that the writer is going to give the reasons for their opinion.

4b   **1** boring **2** follow the same routine **3** stroll **4** hang out with **5** something out of the ordinary **6** check out **7** chill out **8** up for a challenge **9** get out of a rut **10** extreme

4c   **a)** So what is so enjoyable about having a holiday at all?
b) As you can see
c) get out of a rut
d) hang out with/check out/chill out/

5   Sentence a is the best conclusion. It speaks directly to the reader, is amusing.

6   Suggestion: 'Holidays - why bother?'

7   Students' own answers

Boost Your Grade

Listening (pages 40–41)

2   **a)** fun **b)** worked **c)** agents **d)** earn
e) performing **f)** preparation

3   Students' own answers

4a My first experience of the theatre came when I was at college – although my main subjects were English and maths, we all had the chance to <u>have a go at</u> performing arts because it was considered to be good for our personal development. That did it for me. <u>In the beginning</u> I got involved in the technical side of back-stage work and I <u>was particularly keen on</u> doing the lighting. I did that on several college productions.

4b **1** performing arts **2** lighting

5

Jack <u>did not enjoy</u> the (3) .... he had to go to.

According to Jack, it's <u>important</u> for young actors to have a (4) .... to <u>encourage</u> them.

Jack's big break came <u>by chance</u> when a (5) .... saw him in a television advertisement.

Jack <u>is sure that</u> actors must learn the (6) .... as well as their own lines.

Jack <u>uses the word</u> (7)..................... to describe the discussions between actors before a production.

Jack <u>had not expected</u> professional actors to word so hard at (8) ....

Jack <u>felt embarrassed</u> when he had to take a (9) .... on stage instead of the correct prop.

Jack <u>uses the word</u> (10) .... to describe a good performance in a theatre.

6 **3** auditions **4** good agent **5** producer **6** cues
7 workshops **8** basic preparation **9** hat **10** magic

Boost Your Grade

Speaking (pages 42–43)

4 **a)** Students' own answers **b)** No **c)** They didn't talk about spending time with friends. **d)** The man talked about watching sport on TV because he couldn't afford to see it live.

5 **a)** start with **b)** think **c)** what you **d)** mean
e) totally **f)** think **g)** certainly **h)** move **i)** opinion
j) good **k)** personally **l)** partly **m)** view
n) understand **o)** fair **p)** disagree

6

Agreeing	Disagreeing	Asking for opinion	Accepting an opinion	Moving the conversation on
e, g, n	k, l, p	b, d, f, i	c, j, m, o	a, h

Practice Test 2

Reading and Use of English (pages 44–53)

Part 1 (page 44)

1 C **2** D **3** B **4** A **5** D **6** C **7** D **8** C

Part 2 (page 45)

9 be **10** by **11** one **12** our **13** the **14** that **15** for **16** rather

Part 3 (page 46)

17 medical **18** fascination **19** trendy **20** pensioners **21** respectable **22** Inevitably **23** employment **24** irrelevant

Part 4 (page 47)

25 such a difficult test **26** if she knew where her **27** have known Brian for **28** some music instead of watching **29** had had some **30** the first time I have

Part 5 (pages 48–49)

31 D **32** B **33** C **34** A **35** C **36** A

Part 6 (pages 50–51)

37 C **38** A **39** E **40** B **41** D **42** G

Boost your grade! (page 51)

a) sugar **b)** traffic light type symbols
c) people who skip breakfast
d) granola bars and fruit smoothies

Part 7 (pages 52–53)

43 B **44** D **45** A **46** C **47** A **48** C **49** A **50** D **51** B **52** D

Writing (pages 54–55)

Sample answers

Part 1 (page 54)

Some people read a newspaper every day, but is this the best way to find out about what's happening in the news?

Newspapers have articles on a variety of topics like important events, business, sport and celebrities. They provide details that are well-written and interesting for readers. However, because they are printed overnight they are often behind other news outlets such as the internet. Social media sites post information the moment something happens, whereas newspapers may provide 'old news', not 'breaking news'.

On the other hand, newspapers are easy to read and contain articles which express opinions and discuss different points of view. This helps readers make up their mind about what they think about events.

Keeping in touch with the news helps people feel connected to the rest of the world and 24-hour news channels are popular as well as useful for getting both news and views. They are more entertaining than newspapers.

In conclusion, social media and television channels provide information more quickly than newspapers, but the biggest advantage of newspapers is they allow people to take their time and think carefully about what they read.

188 words

Part 2 (page 55)

2

The book 'The Go-between' is set in the past, and tells the story of Leo, a young boy who spends one summer at his school-friend's house in the country. He becomes very fond of his friend's sister Marion, but some dramatic events spoil his happiness and affect the rest of his life.

The book has already been made into a successful film, but this is the first time a musical has been produced. The story follows the events in the book. It is told by the grown-up Leo who is looking back on what happened that summer, and in the musical he is on the stage all the time. All the actors sing well, and the music is played by a single pianist. It reflects the mood of what is happening on stage – sometimes it is happy, sometimes sad. Although I preferred the book, because I could understand more about the characters and why they behave as they do, I found the music very emotional.

I recommend the musical, even if you haven't read the book. The story is easy to follow, and the music is beautiful.

187 words

3

Dear Ms Robbins,

I would like to volunteer for your summer school programme in July. I am keen to experience life abroad and this sounds like an ideal opportunity to do this.

First, to tell you about myself, I am 17 and Swedish. I have a lot of experience with children, as I have three brothers and two sisters and I spend a lot of time doing things with them. I also volunteer at my own school organising after-school activities for the younger students and I enjoy this.

With regard to my own skills, I am good at athletics and during the summer school programme I could help the children improve their running and jumping. I am also good at motivating people to try new things.

I would like to work with people from other countries and I think I could contribute a lot to the summer school. My English is a good standard, as I have been learning for seven years. My only question is about the accommodation: what is it, and how far is it from the summer school?

Looking forward to hearing from you.

187 words

4

A new sports facility

Introduction

This report will give information about current sports facilities in the town, explain why a new sports facility would be useful and recommend which new facility would be best.

Information about current sports facilities

The town has a range of different sports facilities, including a large gym, an indoor swimming pool and an excellent football pitch which is used by many local clubs. However, there are not many opportunities for young people to play a sport together without needing to join a team.

Recommendations

There should be a tennis club in the town, and there are many reasons for this.

- Young people of all ages and abilities can play tennis together
- It is a social sport, so people can meet in the clubhouse and make new friends
- There can be competitions involving people from other towns, which would be fun
- The clubhouse could be used for events for townspeople, such as social evenings
- Tennis courts are not expensive to maintain

For all these reasons, I recommend having a tennis club in the town because it would have many benefits.

189 words

Listening (pages 56–61)

Part 1 (pages 56–57)

1 A **2** B **3** B **4** A **5** C **6** C **7** B **8** B

Part 2 (page 58)

9 vegetarian **10** excitement **11** rural
12 (colourful) markets **13** dramatic **14** conversation
15 games **16** pride **17** cooking **18** songs

Part 3 (page 59)

19 D **20** A **21** E **22** B **23** H

Part 4 (pages 60–61)

24 C **25** A **26** B **27** A **28** B **29** C **30** B

Boost Your Grade

Reading and Use of English (pages 66–67)

1 a

2 **1** … I've now come to realise that it could be rather limiting
2 particularly as I'm not keen on doing some of the more mundane tasks!
3 … though I don't like it I've always accepted that change is certainly not going to happen in the next couple of days!

3 **a)** … though I don't like it I've always accepted that change is certainly not going to happen in the next couple of days!
b) particularly as I'm not keen on doing some of the more mundane tasks!
c) … I've now come to realise that it could be rather limiting

4 **4** B **5** D **6** C **7** E **8** B **9** E **10** C

Boost Your Grade

Writing (pages 68–69)

1 d

3a b – because you are not asked to write about why people want to improve the town, and it is irrelevant in this report

3b and 4

Introduction	Suggestions for Activities	Recommendations
The aim of the report is to say whether the day would be a good idea and suggest activities that could take place.	There could be a quiz about the environment in the evening with prizes. People who live in the town could work in teams to pick up litter. Posters could be put around the town to explain more about recycling.	A day like this is a good idea because it brings people together and creates a town community.

5 d

6 **a)** People who live in the town could work in teams to pick up litter, because there is a lot of litter in the town.
b) Posters could be put up around the town to explain more about recycling, because the landfill site is too big and people need to know more about recycling.
c) There could be a quiz about the environment in the evening with prizes because people don't take environmental problems seriously and need to know more.

7 Suggested answer:

Introduction
The aim of this report is to say whether an English language club would be a good idea, and to suggest activities that could take place in the club.

Suggestions for activities
- There could be a film night once a week where students could watch films in English. This would help them with their listening and improve their vocabulary.
- It would be interesting to have discussion groups or debates in English because speaking is often difficult. If students had a lot of opportunity to speak they would improve quickly.
- Music is a good way to practise pronunciation, so there could be a musical night where students sing songs together in English.

Recommendations
It would be a very good idea to start an English language club in the college, as there are not many opportunities to practise English outside the classroom in the town. I would also recommend opening the club to people who live locally, so that they could also share in the activities.

Boost Your Grade

Listening (pages 70–71)

1   Students' own answers

2   **a)** grateful   **b)** amused   **c)** disappointed   **d)** keen
e) impressed   **f)** nervous   **g)** honoured   **h)** hopeful
i) motivated   **j)** relieved

3a   **1** a   **2** b   **3** b   **4** a   **5** a   **6** b

3b   positive

4   **1** c   **2** d   **3** b   **4** g   **5** h   **6** e   **7** a   **8** f

5   Phrases heard: e, c, h, d, a

6   Speaker 1: 6
Speaker 2: 1
Speaker 3: 5
Speaker 4: 2
Speaker 5: 7

Boost Your Grade

Speaking (pages 72–73)

1   **1** d
2 b
3 e
4 a
5 c

2a   **a** seems to me   **b** never really thought about it
c I feel strongly about   **d** sure that is
e always thought

2b   **1** d   **2** e   **3** a   **4** c   **5** b

3

Interrupting politely	Asking for clarification	Getting your partner to say more
Sorry to interrupt, but..	Sorry, could you say that again?	That's interesting – can you give me an example?
That's a good point, but could I add something?	What did you mean when you said...?	So why do you think that?
Can I say something?	Could you explain what you mean?	Can you say a bit more about that?

4a   Can you say a bit more about that?
Can I say something?

4b   Students' own answers

Practice Test 3

Reading and Use of English (pages 74–83)

Part 1 (page 74)

1 D   **2** B   **3** A   **4** C   **5** D   **6** A   **7** B   **8** D

Part 2 (page 75)

9 or   **10** have   **11** where   **12** if/when   **13** that   **14** up
15 of   **16** a

Part 3 (page 76)

17 affection   **18** sight   **19** recently   **20** disabilities
21 training   **22** tension   **23** speedy   **24** lazily

Part 4 (page 77)

25 'd better   **26** was found by   **27** told Angela to sit down
28 unless dad can drive us   **29** got enough information to
30 have never visited

Part 5 (pages 78–79)

31 B   **32** A   **33** D   **34** C   **35** A   **36** C

Part 6 (pages 80–81)

37 G   **38** D   **39** A   **40** E   **41** B   **42** F

Boost your grade! (page 81)

b) I love skiing
c) a good friend to stop out and walk with me
d) teens who are blind or visually impaired
e) my parents
f) running cross-country

Part 7 (pages 82–83)

43 C   **44** A   **45** D   **46** B   **47** C   **48** B   **49** D   **50** B   **51** A
52 C

Writing (pages 84–85)

Sample answers

Part 1 (page 84)

It's often said that young people watch too much television. However, is this true, and if so, is it a good thing?

Young people lead busy lives and have to deal with different pressures such as taking exams and choosing a career. They must relax in some way, and watching television alone or with friends is one way of doing this. Is this wrong?

Other people choose to spend their leisure time differently, for example playing video games. Technology is part of everyday life and young people often spend hours talking with friends via social media. It is often said that they spend too much time online, and don't actually watch much television.

Clearly, television programmes can be educational, particularly documentaries on topics such as wildlife, and it is good if everyone learns more about these subjects. This is one clear benefit of watching television.

To sum up, everything is a question of balance. In my opinion, young people do not watch too much television because they have many other things to occupy them, but it is important for everyone to do a range of different things in their leisure time.

190 words

Part 2 (page 85)

2

Everyone has some happy memories of their childhood and it's fun to look back on them. Some moments stand out more than others though, and in my case it is a sporting achievement.

I had always wanted to be in the local junior tennis team but was never considered good enough, although I spent ages practising my technique. I loved playing at the local club, and hanging out with my friends there. Then, one day I was watching a match when the captain came up to me and said 'Jenny can't play the next match – can you stand in'? I was terrified, but said yes and rushed to get my racquet. The match was hard, but I felt inspired – I won, and everyone was so pleased with me. I'd never felt so proud of myself!

Moments like that can be life-changing, and it gave me more confidence generally. It was not only good for my tennis, but for other parts of my life too. It also taught me how important it is to make the most of every opportunity, so doesn't that make it an important moment?

187 words

3

Hi Carlos,

Great news that you're coming to the music festival! It's going to be really good this year because the main band is Red Apples, and they're excellent – you must know them because they stream loads of their music.

You can get tickets online but they don't go on sale until 9am next Friday. You should register on the festival website now though, so you can get them more easily on Friday. Don't forget that the festival is on Saturday and Sunday, so you'll need to buy a ticket for both days.

Hotels get very busy when the festival is on, and are expensive too, but that's not a problem for you because you can stay at my house. I live quite near the stadium so getting to the festival is easy. I'd love to be able to spend time with you, and we can go to the concerts together. I can show you round the town one afternoon – there's a lovely walk along by the river that we can do if the weather is good.

Let's arrange everything once you've got your tickets.

See you soon!

188 words

4

Reading is important to me, and I like reading all kinds of books. One book I really enjoyed was 'Lord of the Flies'. The story is about a group of boys who survive a plane crash and live on an isolated island, and how they behave when they are so far from civilisation and there are no adults to tell them what to do. The story is exciting, because although the boys behave well at the start, what happens later is unexpected, and the violence is shocking. Some of the scenes are very dramatic, and are well written.

There are some interesting characters in the book, particularly Ralph who is seen as a good person. Piggy is a very complicated character who tries to do good, but he has a difficult time and the reader feels very sorry for him. I think that it is the personal reaction I had to these characters that makes the book so memorable.

I recommend this book not only because it is exciting and interesting, but because it made me think about how people get on with each other and how we should behave.

190 words

Listening (pages 86–91)

Part 1 (pages 86–87)

1 B **2** A **3** C **4** C **5** A **6** B **7** A **8** A

Part 2 (page 88)

9 Iron Way **10** (steel) cables / cables made of steel **11** views **12** helmet **13** goats **14** dizzy **15** risky **16** giants **17** proud **18** animals

Part 3 (page 89)

19 C **20** D **21** E **22** H **23** G

Boost your grade! (page 89)

a) capable **b)** messing about **c)** seriously **d)** society
e) broadens

Part 4 (pages 90–91)

24 C **25** B **26** A **27** C **28** C **29** A **30** B

Boost your grade! (page 91)

1	**1** a **2** c **3** b **4** a **5** b **6** a **7** b

3	The correct option is C: Carly says 'it seemed a thrilling thing to get involved in' which has a very similar meaning to 'she thought it would be an exciting thing to take part in'.

Option A is not correct because Carly talks about what she is capable of doing (acrobatics) but she doesn't mention wanting to show these skills to other people.

Option B is not correct. Carly talks about 'the TV competition' and 'before', but actually says she hadn't paid any attention to it.

4	The correct answer is Option A. She says that she'd 'better get my ideas together', which indicates that she needs to do something for the future. The option says 'still had a lot of hard work to do' (in the future).

Option B is wrong: 'seriously considered quitting' is a distractor, but Carly says she never seriously considered this, meaning she wanted to continue in the competition.

Option C is incorrect – 'although ... delighted to have got through' is misleading – she was pleased to get into the next round, but she doesn't mention that this was more than she had expected.

Practice Test 4

Reading and Use of English (pages 96–105)

Part 1 (page 96)

1 C **2** D **3** A **4** B **5** C **6** D **7** A **8** B

Part 2 (page 97)

9 by **10** them **11** is **12** being **13** Another **14** come
15 as **16** found

Part 3 (page 98)

17 qualification **18** profitable **19** especially
20 employer **21** addition **22** disadvantages
23 acceptable **24** actually

Part 4 (page 99)

25 wish (that) I had gone **26** had been closed by
27 was allowed to **28** have been working
29 put off (doing) **30** so that he would not

Part 5 (pages 100–101)

31 D **32** B **33** A **34** C **35** B **36** C

Part 6 (pages 102–103)

37 G **38** C **39** A **40** D **41** B **42** F

Part 7 (pages 104–105)

43 C **44** A **45** B **46** A **47** C **48** B **49** D **50** B **51** D
52 C

Writing (pages 106–107)

Part 1 (page 106)

Cities are important places for business and entertainment, so they are busy. Heavy traffic causes problems, but is the answer to ban private cars from them completely?

On the one hand, banning cars reduces pollution. In some cities pollution levels are so high that people can become ill. If cars were banned, the air would become cleaner and people's lives would be healthier.

On the other hand, people need to get into cities for work, shopping and entertainment, and cycling or walking may be impossible. A city must have a good system of public transport in place before banning cars. In some places people can park outside the city and take a bus into the centre, which is a good solution.

However, one big problem is that people like cars. They feel comfortable driving them, and don't want to exchange them for a longer ride on a tram or bus. They want to drive into the city centre.

In conclusion, it probably is a good idea to cut down on cars in city centres, but banning them completely could be expensive and unpopular.

183 words

Part 2 (page 107)

2

A lot of the time people spend on the internet is wasted because they browse websites that are not useful. However, that's not the case with one particular website I often use.

It's a website called Sport Life. It is basically a site with information on keeping fit and healthy, tips for improving training techniques and links to shopping sites where you can buy your sports kit.

Why is it so useful? It's really well set-out and user-friendly, and it's easy to find everything. The tips are written by experts, but are easy to understand and follow – they are also updated regularly so you are always learning something new. The links take you to excellent shopping sites which have special offers. The best thing is the message board, where people can share their experiences and ask for advice. In this way you can get in touch with people who share your interest in sport. Finally, there are advertisements for special sports competitions that anyone can enter.

I recommend the website, especially for anyone just starting to think about doing more sport. Why not try it?

185 words

3

A language course

Introduction

The aim of this report is to describe a language course I took in Spain, and make recommendations about it.

The course

The intensive course lasted for two weeks, and was for intermediate students. One advantage was the small classes of only around ten people. The teachers were excellent and gave us lots of chances to practise speaking. I learned a lot of new vocabulary and became much more confident in my listening ability.

I lived with a host family and they were very kind. We had dinner together every night, and they helped me a lot with my pronunciation.

Recommendations

This is a good course for anyone who already speaks some of the language, although it would be hard for beginners. I recommend staying with a family, because you get a really good idea of everyday life in the country, and you make some good friends. I am still in contact with both the family I stayed with and other students in my class.

The biggest advantage is being able to live in a different country for a short time, and I recommend it.

189 words

4

Could I live without sport? That's an interesting question which I shall try to answer.

As long as I can remember my family have been interested in sport. My grandfather took me to watch football when I was very young. My father played tennis, and my mother was keen on swimming. With so much sport in my childhood, you'd expect me to follow their example, but I didn't. I loved music, and I ignored their attempts to interest me in sport. It wasn't until I went to secondary school that I discovered the fun of playing hockey in a team. I also discovered that I was good at it, and that helped a lot!

In fact, it started everything. I needed to be fit to play hockey, so I started running. Then I took up swimming, and joined a gym. I made many new friends, and found that I felt healthier and happier when I was doing sport.

Playing a team sport like hockey is best, because it's fun. Could I live without it? The answer is no, not now, and actually I would not want to try.

188 words

Listening (pages 108–113)

Part 1 (pages 108–109)

1 A **2** B **3** C **4** A **5** A **6** B **7** A **8** C

Part 2 (page 110)

9 keen **10** practice **11** folk group **12** website
13 basement **14** Red Mist **15** cover **16** festival
17 wedding **18** agent

Part 3 (page 111)

19 H **20** E **21** C **22** G **23** F

Part 4 (pages 112–113)

24 C **25** B **26** C **27** C **28** B **29** A **30** A

Boost your grade! (page 113)

1   **1** eight **2** one **3** three **4** twice **5** two **6** three
  7 ten **8** exact **9** five **10** each **11** eight **12** one
  13 seven **14** three **15** same **16** each

CAMBRIDGE ENGLISH
Language Assessment
Part of the University of Cambridge

Do not write in this box

Candidate Name
If not already printed, write name
in CAPITALS and complete the
Candidate No. grid (in pencil).

Candidate Signature

Examination Title

Centre

Supervisor:
If the candidate is ABSENT or has WITHDRAWN shade here ☐

Centre No.

Candidate No.

Examination
Details

Candidate Answer Sheet

Instructions

Use a PENCIL (B or HB).

Rub out any answer you wish
to change using an eraser.

Parts 1, 5, 6 and 7:
Mark ONE letter for each
question.

For example, if you think **B** is the right
answer to the question, mark your
answer sheet like this:

0 ☐A☐ ■B■ ☐C☐ ☐D☐

Parts 2, 3 and 4:
Write your answer clearly
in CAPITAL LETTERS.

For Parts 2 and 3 write one letter
in each box. For example:

0 E X A M P L E

Part 1

	A	B	C	D
1	A	B	C	D
2	A	B	C	D
3	A	B	C	D
4	A	B	C	D
5	A	B	C	D
6	A	B	C	D
7	A	B	C	D
8	A	B	C	D

Part 2

Do not write here

9	1 0 u
10	1 0 u
11	1 0 u
12	1 0 u
13	1 0 u
14	1 0 u
15	1 0 u
16	1 0 u

Continues over

DP802

Part 3

Do not write below here

17	1 0 u
18	1 0 u
19	1 0 u
20	1 0 u
21	1 0 u
22	1 0 u
23	1 0 u
24	1 0 u

Part 4

Do not write below here

25	2 1 0 u
26	2 1 0 u
27	2 1 0 u
28	2 1 0 u
29	2 1 0 u
30	2 1 0 u

Part 5

31	A	B	C	D
32	A	B	C	D
33	A	B	C	D
34	A	B	C	D
35	A	B	C	D
36	A	B	C	D

Part 6

37	A	B	C	D	E	F	G
38	A	B	C	D	E	F	G
39	A	B	C	D	E	F	G
40	A	B	C	D	E	F	G
41	A	B	C	D	E	F	G
42	A	B	C	D	E	F	G

Part 7

43	A	B	C	D	E	F
44	A	B	C	D	E	F
45	A	B	C	D	E	F
46	A	B	C	D	E	F
47	A	B	C	D	E	F
48	A	B	C	D	E	F
49	A	B	C	D	E	F
50	A	B	C	D	E	F
51	A	B	C	D	E	F
52	A	B	C	D	E	F

denote PRINT LIMITED 0121 520 5100

FCE R

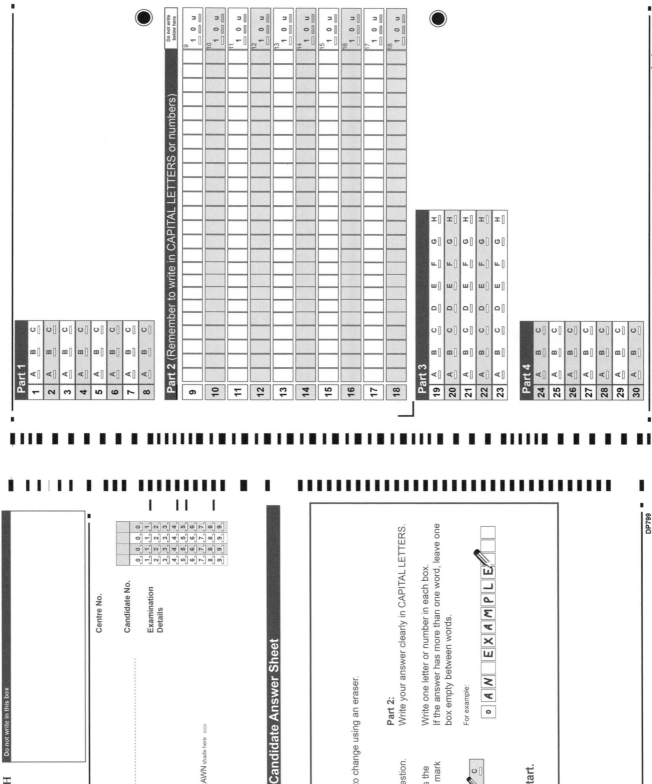

Authors: Helen Chilton, Lynda Edwards, Jacky Newbrook

Additional material: Sarah Curtis

Publisher: Jacquie Bloese

Editor: Sarah Curtis

Design: Oxford Designers & Illustrators Ltd

Cover Design: Nicolle Thomas

Picture Research: Suzanne Williams

Picture credits:

Page 11: Portra/iStockphoto.

Page 13: Image Source, B.Van Der Meer/Getty Images.

Page 20: O.Ortakcioglu/iStockphoto.

Page 28: sturti/iStockphoto.

Page 33: E.Meitzel, M.Rakusen/Getty Images.

Page 34: Hero Images, RoBeDeRo/Getty Images.

Page 43: asiseeit/iStockphoto.

Page 50: cerealphotos/iStockphoto.

Page 58: FatCamera, hadynyah/iStockphoto.

Page 63: Plume Creative, W.Perugini/Getty Images.

Page 64: S.Kawamoto/Getty Images, B.Thorne/
Bloomberg via Getty Images.

Page 88: photobac/iStockphoto.

Page 93: kerkla, L.Arvidsson/Getty Images.

Page 94: ducation Images/UIG via Getty Images,
J.Harper/Getty Images.

Page 102: M.L.Pearson/Alamy Stock Photo.

Page 110: hjalmeida/iStockphoto.

Page 115: J.Swain, S.Marcus/Getty Images.

Page 116: Hero Images, Westend61/Getty Images.

**The publishers are grateful for permission from
Scholastic Inc., for use of the following articles and
data:**

'Should Teens Do Extreme Sports?' (Choices, October
2016); 'How healthy are you ... Really?' (Choices,
September 2016); 'Noah is Blind' (Choices, November /
December 2016); 'Shanice is a Native American' (Choices,
April 2015); 'Are Online Friends Real Friends?' (Choices,
September 2016); 'Break a Bad Habit in 5' (Choices,
January 2016)

Printed in the UK by Bell and Bain Ltd, Glasgow